GW01459240

Eyewitness at Dieppe

Eyewitness at Dieppe

Ross Reyburn

PEN & SWORD
HISTORY

First published in Great Britain in 2022 by
Pen & Sword History
An imprint of
Pen & Sword Books Ltd
Yorkshire – Philadelphia

ISBN 978 1 39905 997 8

A CIP catalogue record for this book is available from the British Library.

Typeset by Mac Style
Printed in the UK by CPI Group (UK) Ltd, Croydon, CR0 4YY.

MIX
Paper from
responsible sources
FSC www.fsc.org FSC® C013604

Pen & Sword Books Limited incorporates the imprints of Atlas, Archaeology, Aviation, Discovery, Family History, Fiction, History, Maritime, Military, Military Classics, Politics, Select, Transport, True Crime, Air World, Frontline Publishing, Leo Cooper, Remember When, Seaforth Publishing, The Praetorian Press, Wharncliffe Local History, Wharncliffe Transport, Wharncliffe True Crime and White Owl.

For a complete list of Pen & Sword titles please contact

PEN & SWORD BOOKS LIMITED
47 Church Street, Barnsley, South Yorkshire, S70 2AS, England
E-mail: enquiries@pen-and-sword.co.uk
Website: www.pen-and-sword.co.uk

Or

PEN AND SWORD BOOKS
1950 Lawrence Rd, Havertown, PA 19083, USA
E-mail: Uspen-and-sword@casematepublishers.com
Website: www.penandswordbooks.com

*Our nation's children are remembrance's hope. If they
do not learn why a generation of young people with hopes
and dreams of their own set those aside to fight a noble war
in faraway lands, then an essential national memory will fade
and die away. And Canada will be the poorer for it. So it
behoves us all to keep that memory alive.*

Canadian historian Mark Zuehlke concluding his book
Tragedy at Dieppe: Operation Jubilee, August 19, 1942 (2012)

Contents

PART ONE

A Fortunate Survivor

By freelance journalist Ross Reyburn, eldest son of the late Wallace Reyburn (1913–2001).

On 19 August 1942, my father crossed the English Channel before dawn broke, spent six and a half hours on French soil and then returned to England.

He was very fortunate to get back alive relatively unscathed, for 3,367 of the 4,963 Canadian soldiers involved in the ill-fated Dieppe Raid that Wallace Reyburn covered as a Canadian war correspondent for the *Montreal Standard* were casualties, with their final death total numbering 907. A total of 1,946 were taken prisoner.

Awarded an OBE for his bravery as the only war correspondent ashore, his book *Rehearsal for Invasion: An Eyewitness Story of the Dieppe Raid*, a wartime bestseller, was first published by George G. Harrap & Co. Ltd in 1943.

Many historians and academics have recorded and passed judgment on the biggest disaster in Canadian military history, but Reyburn's book remains the only account of what it was actually like to be alongside the Canadians taking part in the raid from start to finish and witnessing the street fighting first-hand.

With a journalist's eye for the telling anecdote, he provided a vivid, often harrowing account of being a civilian for the first time in a battle situation where too many of the Canadian soldiers he went ashore with were killed in the face of unequal odds. Alongside the earliest troops to hit the shoreline in the raid, he was also aboard the last ship to return to England.

He offered an invaluable insight into the minds of Canadian troops at Dieppe, who deserve to be remembered for bravely fighting a losing battle against far superior firepower ('It was like answering a cannon with a pop-gun') after voluntarily leaving the safety of their homeland to risk their lives fighting a dictator responsible for exterminating millions and overrunning a vast swathe of Europe.

Defeat it may have been, but he did not find it hard to find examples of heroism among the Canadian troops facing the burden of being asked to overcome a far superior armed and deployed enemy.

* * *

He witnessed Lieutenant Colonel Cecil Merritt winning Canada's first VC of the war, ignoring heavy enemy fire and leading his troops over the bridge at Pourville time and time again. The bravado of others he encountered was also dutifully recorded. Men such as Private Charlie Sawden from the Saskatchewan prairies, who when quizzed about his pre-war career grinned and told my father to just put him down as 'a horse thief'.

Fortunate to avoid being among Dieppe's dead after witnessing over six hours of fighting in the streets of Pourville and on the shoreline, Reyburn took an age in which he survived two boat sinkings to get from the beach onto the headquarters ship HMS *Calpe* in the withdrawal. Then followed three hours of nerve-wracking suspense, wondering if the destroyer he was on would survive attacks by enemy planes before it finally headed back to England after ensuring the withdrawal from the beaches was completed.

Written under the limitations of wartime censorship, the early part of Reyburn's narrative contains a detailed justification for the raid, titled Operation Jubilee, masterminded by Combined Operations chief Lord Louis Mountbatten ostensibly as a try-out for D-Day, testing what it would be like landing troops on the French coast against German defences. He also hailed a victory won in the air battle as 'an outstanding achievement'.

The latter viewpoint is totally contradicted by statistics viewed in detail that showed initial estimates of enemy planes downed were wildly inaccurate. The RAF paid a heavy price at Dieppe, for 67 airmen were listed as killed or presumed dead while 106 Allied aircraft were lost, the highest single day total of the war. By comparison, the Luftwaffe officially listed only 48 of their planes suffering the same fate.

The only unqualified success of the Dieppe Raid was provided by the battle-hardened British No. 4 Commando. Under the inspirational leadership of the dashing Lord Lovat, they destroyed the entire artillery battery of six 150-millimetre Krupp guns at Varengeville. While No. 3 Commando, with their attack plans in disarray, failed to destroy the coastal battery at Berneval, they managed to cause enough mayhem to limit its effectiveness during the raid.

In the book, Reyburn's analysis of the reasons for attacking a strongly defended port on the French coast as a reconnaissance raid backed Mountbatten's carefully constructed, self-serving verdict on the raid. In September 1962, in the Canadian Broadcasting Corporation documentary, *Close Up*, marking the twentieth anniversary of Operation Jubilee, Mountbatten produced his ultimate justification for the death toll at Dieppe brazenly claiming:

The old Duke of Wellington has been credited with saying that the Battle of Waterloo was won on the playing fields of Eton. I am quite sure that the Battle of Normandy was won on the beaches of Dieppe. For every man who died in Dieppe, at least ten more must have been spared in Normandy in 1944.

Less edifying was Mountbatten's remark made not long before his death in 1979 at the hands of the IRA blowing up his fishing boat off the Irish coast, when he said of the reaction of Canadians to their heavy losses at Dieppe: 'They want to revel in their misery.' But this remark should not necessarily be interpreted as indifference to the realities of warfare or what one critic perceptively termed the well-connected Mountbatten's 'aristocratic insouciance'.

He may have been a reckless commander, but no one questioned his bravery commanding the destroyer HMS *Kelly*, which was eventually sunk by enemy aircraft during the Battle of Crete in 1941.

His rapid promotion as a key figure in the Allied planning hierarchy heading Combined Operations Headquarters and given the task of ultimately ending the war was not sought by him; he had asked to return to active duty to be reportedly met with Prime Minister Winston Churchill's laconic reply: 'What could you hope to achieve there except to be sunk in a bigger and more expensive ship next time?'

Mountbatten was all too aware you had to accept there was an inevitable price in terms of casualties to pay for fighting a war against a formidable enemy. In the aftermath of Dieppe, Canada's first VC of the war, Lieutenant Colonel Merritt, shared the same fatalistic view saying: 'We were very glad to go, we were delighted. We were up against a very difficult situation, and we didn't win. But to hell with this business of saying the generals done us dirt.'

But the reality was that Operation Jubilee (which went ahead after the original plan – titled Operation Rutter – had been abandoned on 7 July due to bad weather) was an ill-conceived battleplan. Examine the plethora of authoritative books detailing the many aspects of the planning process resulting in that final blueprint for the raid and you find common sense taking a backseat. There was only one victor in such a foolhardy enterprise – the Germans.

In his masterful, superbly researched account of the raid, *Tragedy at Dieppe* (2012), Canadian historian Mark Zuehlke details just how such a flawed plan of sending some 6,100 troops across the Channel in 245 vessels to a heavily defended French port gained unstoppable momentum.

* * *

Mountbatten's role as the key figure responsible for what happened to the Canadians at Dieppe heading Combined Operations Headquarters is not as clear-cut as it might seem. There was ever-increasing backing for a Second Front to be opened up by the Allies in Western Europe to ease the Soviet Union's horrific burden fighting the German invaders on the killing fields of the Eastern Front, coupled with restless

Canadian forces in England who were clamouring for a chance to fight the enemy, proved key factors resulting in the final plan.

As Zuehlke relates, Mountbatten in vain originally tried to avoid Canadian troops being involved as the main attacking force arguing: 'We were bound to have heavy casualties ... this was the very last operation on which untried and inexperienced Canadian troops should be used.'

Concerns that Russia might make peace with the Germans, and pressure from the Britain's American ally catapulted into the war by the Japanese attack on Pearl Harbor in December 1941, were other factors resulting in formulating a major operation in mainland Europe despite the UK's limited military resources.

Nevertheless, as I knew all too well from talking to my father about his wartime experiences, and free from propaganda restrictions, he reversed his justification for the raid in his book and unequivocally blamed Mountbatten for the disaster that was Dieppe.

On 27 August 1967, as the twenty-fifth anniversary of the raid was commemorated, he made this view public sending a scathing letter to the *Sunday Telegraph* condemning Mountbatten (see Appendix II).

In his biography *Mountbatten: Apprentice Warlord 1900–1943* (2010), Adrian Smith referring to this letter wrote:

In Britain the thin veil of discretion was seriously torn apart in the summer of 1967 when Wallace Reyburn wrote to the Sunday Telegraph bitterly denouncing Mountbatten's claim that Dieppe was a vital prerequisite for D-Day. No longer the dutiful propagandist, Reyburn recalled his own horrific experiences on Green Beach in a remarkable letter, which lambasted everyone connected with organizing the raid. With iconoclastic candour and lack of deference, he tore into Mountbatten – here was a man unapologetic over sacrificing more than 1,000 lives in order to learn lessons which his staff could quiet easily have worked out for themselves.

However, Mountbatten's viewpoint justifying the raid was not without its influential supporters. In 1950, the fourth volume of Winston

Churchill's history *The Second World War* was published. Titled *The Hinge of Fate*, Britain's great wartime prime minister justified the high cost of the raid:

> *I thought it most important that a large-scale operation should take place that summer and military opinion seemed unanimous that until an operation of that scale was undertaken no responsible general would take the responsibility of planning for the main invasion…*
>
> *The Canadian Army in Britain had long been eager and impatient for action… Although the utmost gallantry and devotion were shown by all the troops and British Commandos and by the landing-craft and their escorts, and many splendid deeds were done, the results were disappointing and the casualties very heavy. In the Canadian 2nd Division 18 per cent of the five thousand men embarked lost their lives and nearly two thousand were taken prisoners.*
>
> *Looking back, the casualties of this memorable action may seem out of proportion to the results. It would be wrong to judge the episode solely by such a standard. Dieppe occupies a place of its own in the story of the war, and the grim casualty figures must not class it as a failure.*
>
> *Tactically it was a mine of experience, It shed revealing light on many shortcomings in our outlook It taught us to build in good time various new types of craft and appliances for later use. We learnt again the value of powerful support by heavy naval guns in an opposed landing, and our bombardment technique, both marine and aerial, was thereafter improved. Above all it was shown that individual skill and gallantry without thorough organization and combined training would not prevail, and that teamwork was the secret of success. This could only be provided by trained and organized amphibious formations. All these lessons were taken to heart.*
>
> *Strategically the raid served to make the Germans more conscious of the danger along the whole coast of Occupied France. This helped to hold troops and resources in the West, which did something to take the weight off Russia. Honour to the brave who fell, Their sacrifice was not in vain.*

Churchill's account of the raid did not mention an important factor that heightened the raid's failure. Speculation that the Germans had some prior knowledge of the raid proved a misconception when their records were examined in the post-war years. However, their estimate of the threat to the Dieppe sector had led to their significantly strengthening their defences along the whole of this coastline across the Channel from England. When the raid struck, the division responsible for the defence of the Dieppe area was at full strength having been reinforced during July and August in the weeks prior to the raid and was on routine alert.

The reality of Dieppe experienced first-hand by my father was somewhat starker than Churchill's view. Put in the simplest terms, the fact Canadian troops could not match the firepower directed at them was evidenced by casualty figures and the huge numbers ending up as prisoners of war.

Lord Lovat, operating on the right flank of the main operation, shared my father's view that the Canadian troops engaged in the frontal assault on the resort's three breaches faced an 'impossible' task.

In the CBC documentary *Close Up*, Lovat stated with pinpoint clarity: 'The defences of Dieppe town and harbour were impregnable, no matter how well trained you were. And that I'm sure of. Nobody could have taken Dieppe.'

The contrasting roles of two Dieppe heroes – Lord Lovat and Lieutenant Colonel Ces Merritt – captured the enormity of the battle task facing the Canadians.

The charismatic Lovat, later immortalized for his D-Day heroics guiding his commandos ashore at Sword Beach to the sound of the bagpipes played by his personal piper Bill Mullin, was a leader in the Errol Flynn mould described by Churchill as 'the handsomest man to cut a throat'.

After scaling cliffs, his commandos engaged in bitter hand-to-hand fighting and silenced every gun battery at Varengeville, ensuring they were unable to fire at at the Canadian troops hitting the beaches.

Ces Merritt's heroics witnessed first-hand by my father were equally awe-inspiring. However, time and time again, guiding his men through heavy enemy fire over the bridge at Pourville, unlike silencing the German guns at Varengeville, held no great military significance and merely showed the Canadian troops were tackling far superior firepower.

Perhaps the most telling condemnation of the futility of the operation came from those facing the attack. As Zuehlke recalls in his book, the 302nd Infantry Division's commander, Generalleutnant Konrad Haase, found it 'incomprehensible' that it was believed the troops sent to Dieppe would be able to 'overrun a Germany Infantry Regiment reinforced with artillery'.

He also praised the 'great energy' of the Canadians, listing their failure as not for 'the lack of courage' but the result of the 'concentrated defensive fire' they had to overcome.

The reality was this was a doomed reconnaissance in force however experienced the soldiers taking part were. While the number of Allied troops, sailors and airmen killed totalled 1,227, German army losses list 322 killed and 280 wounded.

While he later contradicted his wartime book verdict on the planners, Reyburn's account of his own role in the Dieppe Raid, portraying the realities of experiencing battle for the first time and laden with 'What the hell is going to happen next?' and 'Will I get out of this alive?' thoughts echoed the reality of combat.

True, you can find factual errors linked to his own experiences in the book, misleadingly titled *Glorious Chapter: The Canadians at Dieppe* (London: G. G. Harrap & Co. Ltd; Toronto: Oxford University Press, 1943) and also more accurately *Dawn Landing* (Digit Books, 1958) in its two other editions.

My father was misinformed when he wrote in 1943 that Charlie Sawden, one of the many men he talked to during the raid, was 'walking about in England today without a scratch on him'. You can find the South Saskatchewan soldier's grave in the Canadian War Cemetery near Dieppe as he died during the beach withdrawal with a leg shattered by a bullet after his heroic exploit tossing two grenades into a pillbox and killing the German soldiers manning the fortification.

But these errors don't detract from the fact that the aim of his narrative – 'I have tried to give a frank account of how it feels to step out everyday life and go with an invading force undertaking a raid' – was evocatively fulfilled.

My father never regarded his role reporting the raid as in any way heroic and he was quite happy to refer to the often-quoted general description of the OBE medal he received being given to recipients for 'Other Buggers' Efforts'.

He also made light of the fact he numbered among the vast number of Allied casualties in the raid – around 75 per cent of those taking part. During the action, he felt his battledress trousers were damp with sweat. It was only later he found that what he thought was sweat was actually blood as shrapnel fragments had hit his buttocks resulting in a minor hospital operation after his return to England.

While he later reversed his justification of the raid and facts that emerged after the war contradicted propaganda-inspired reports in the immediate aftermath of the raid, he never viewed his account of the events in the raid that he actually experienced as a distortion

While Wallace Reyburn was a gifted storyteller, he regarded what he wrote of the Dieppe Raid as an important authentic tribute to the bravery of the Canadian troops facing a senseless task.

One was reminded of Field Marshal Harold Alexander's view: 'As regards propaganda, I feel it is the best policy to tell the truth – when it helps you.' While the scripts of many acclaimed war films may have taken liberties with the truth, there was no need to exaggerate the reality that turned the Dieppe Raid into a disaster.

Many others besides Reyburn bore witness to the bravery of Ces Merritt on that bridge at Pourville that was renamed Merritt's Bridge in his honour. His reckless bravery was there for all to see when he remained behind fighting a rearguard action to help protect soldiers under fire during the hectic evacuation.

Merritt's war ended at Dieppe when he eventually surrendered as his ammunition ran out. He spent the remaining three years of the conflict as a prisoner of war. Back in Canada, his wife, Grace Merritt, sent my father a cable asking if he had any news of her husband after reading his account of Merritt's heroics in the *Montreal Standard*. Later, he visited her Ontario home to describe what he had witnessed in person.

Reyburn's attack on a fellow war correspondent covering the raid offered another indication that what he witnessed first-hand at Dieppe should be faithfully recorded. Quentin Reynolds, the American journalist writing for *Collier's Weekly*, spent the entire raid aboard the headquarters ship HMS *Calpe* and later published a book titled *Dress Rehearsal: The Story of Dieppe* (New York: Blue Ribbon Books, 1943).

In his second book about his Second World War experiences, *Some Of It Was Fun*, published by the Toronto firm Thomas Nelson & Sons in 1949, Reyburn produced a scathing verdict on the Quentin Reynolds book on the raid:

> *The war correspondent who didn't have at least one war-time book to his credit was pretty much the exception. A high proportion of the books were of the type in which the writer gave the readers at home the inside story of how he could have waged a certain battle much more effectively than the generals. Such a book was Quentin Reynolds' about the Dieppe Raid – 'Dress Rehearsal'. So warped was Reynolds' view of this battle and such a distortion that the British would far rather have seen it not published. When the British censors read it in London, numerous conferences were held at which the British chiefs of staff pondered how they could prevent such a mis-statement of fact from reaching the public. But censorship at that time was merely for military purposes – matters of policy were never censored. Provided the writer didn't give away military secrets, he could say what he liked.*

Reyburn's own account offered an insight into his ability to witness events with a journalistic eye for the striking observation, such as his sighting the French farmer calmly herding his cows in a field oblivious to the German mortar fire passing above him directed at the invading force.

He also laid bare any misconception that the inexperienced Canadian soldiers came second best because their German opponents were superior fighters rather than the reality that they faced an impossible task against far superior weaponry.

German prisoners were taken by the troops he was with but later set free as the wounded took priority in the final evacuation. Reyburn noted the striking contrast between the powerfully built young Canadians while the Nazis were 'of poor physique' and mostly 'either old or very young', providing evidence that the German army's best troops were on the brutal Russian front.

He never regarded his role in the raid as anything more than an observer as a guest of the South Saskatchewan Regiment narrating the reality of experiencing the reality of warfare for the first time. I can remember quizzing my father about the shrapnel wound in his rear he received witnessing the street battles and getting the matter-of-fact reply: 'I was sitting on a rock having a cigarette when a German sniper got me in the backside.' The reality was very different as he narrates in the book.

My own family links to the Dieppe Raid are not limited to my father for I was given the first name of my uncle Ross Munro, the Canadian press lead war correspondent in Europe in the Second World War. He too was at Dieppe; my mother was his younger sister Betty Munro, whom my father married after divorcing his first wife. Unlike my father, who was able to scramble up Pourville beach with the first troops to hit the shoreline untroubled by enemy fire on the raid's right flank while the Germans were largely asleep, Munro was with the Royal Regiment of Canada arriving on the other side of the central landing site on the beach at Dieppe itself, at Puys, after being fatally delayed by a brief skirmish with an enemy convoy in the Channel.

Landing late without cover of darkness, they found the enemy on full alert manning the guns on the high cliffs flanking either side of the narrow, vulnerable beach at the small seaside resort. Puys provided a far smaller but equally futile Canadian version of that harrowing first day of the Battle of the Somme in 1916 when 20,000 British troops were killed by machine-gun fire attacking the enemy across no man's land.

Viewing the scene below the cliffs at Puys, it is difficult to imagine a less favourable beach setting for landing troops in a combat situation. Soldiers in the Royal Regiment were obliterated with 227 out of a force of 543 killed.

Munro witnessed the slaughter from the stern of a landing craft and after the war, somewhat absurdly, was labelled 'a coward' by Private Joe Ryan, a Royal survivor in the same landing craft, for not following the soldiers around him in their doomed attack.

When the ramp fell, the leading troops 'plunged into about two feet of water and machine-gun bullets laced into them,' Munro wrote after the raid. 'Bodies piled up on the ramp. Some staggered to the beach and fell. Bullets were splattering into the boat wounding and killing. Looking out the open bow over the bodies I saw a slope leading up to a stone wall littered with Royal casualties. There must have been sixty or seventy of them lying sprawled... On no other front have I witnessed such carnage.'

In 1962, Terence Robertson in his controversial book, *Dieppe: The Shame and the Glory*, accused Royal Regiment of Canada soldiers of cowardice at Puys.

Reviewing the book in a CBC interview (see Appendix I) in a studio at the BBC headquarters at Bush House in London, my father provided a moving defence of the Royals.

The Canadian operation at Pourville proved hazardous enough but he was fortunate to be following the least disastrous of the three beach attacks in the raid. Blessed with the element of surprise, he was with the first South Saskatchewan Regiment soldiers scrambling ashore untroubled by the enemy. But with an enemy alerted manning formidable defences, it was a very different story later on the resort's main beach while the slaughter on the other flank at Puys proved horrific.

'I was over there the other day having another look at Puys beach where they landed,' he said in the broadcast. 'And when I stood there looking at it from the enemy's point of view I could only shake my head. The Royals you see had a dirty job all right. The thing was worse than just a dirty job.

'It was absolutely ridiculous, foolhardy to the point of being suicidal.

'Personally I wouldn't for a second stand in judgment on any member of the Royal Regiment for being hesitant when given as his first taste of battle such a suicidal assignment.'

Reyburn also provided a defence on behalf of General J. H. 'Ham' Roberts, the conscientious army commander handling the Canadian troops, who was made a scapegoat for the disaster.

It is easy to sympathize with Roberts as he was given control of what was an impossible mission. But although his role masterminding events from the headquarters destroyer, HMS *Calpe*, was handicapped by an inadequate signals network producing contradictory messages from the troops ashore, he made the fatal mistake of sending reserve units onto the main beach at Dieppe after the main attack had failed to achieve its objective of getting troops, supported by tanks, into the town itself.

In the words of former foreign correspondent Patrick Bishop in his absorbing account of the raid. *Operation Jubilee: Dieppe 1942: The Folly and the Sacrifice* (Penguin Viking, 2021):

Roberts violated a cardinal military perception so commonplace and obvious that it was widely known to civilians, He was reinforcing failure and doing it twice.

The consequences of this misguided leadership did not match the horrific casualty count earlier on the beach at Puys the far side of the main town. But it was a similar exercise in futility.

Roberts, contradicting what he could view some three miles offshore aboard HMS *Calpe*, decided to send the Les Fusiliers Mont-Royal ashore. Facing overwhelming odds, 119 soldiers in the Montréal-based French Canadian regiment were killed and another 344 taken prisoner. Only 125 made it back to England and four of those died from their wounds.

Amidst this carnage, Lieutenant Colonel Dollard Ménard proved an inspirational figure, awarded the DSO (Distinguished Service Order) for displaying in the words of the medal citation, 'the highest qualities of courage and leadership' leading his battalion despite being wounded five times before he finally passed out and was evacuated on an LCA.

The folly was compounded on a lesser scale when a second reserve unit, the Royal Marines, were sent ashore with the landing craft bombarded by enemy fire and ordered to re-embark ten minutes after hitting the shoreline with twenty-four left dead.

The Marine commandos only avoided a far higher death toll because Lieutenant Colonel Joseph Picton Phillips, after bravely directing landing craft onto the beach in plain sight of the enemy, realized his troops would be slaughtered and stood on the stern of his LCM waving to the boats trailing astern to turn back into the cover of a smokescreen. As the boats began to turn round he was shot and died a few minutes later.

No Allied war photographer survived the raid to return to England with photographs of the battle ashore. But the German propaganda photographs taken after the raid revealed the true extent of the disaster, showing the bodies of the Royals lying sprawled in front of the sea wall at Puys, the burnt-out tanks that never reached the streets of the town lying stranded on the resort's main beach and the masses of Canadian troops herded up as prisoners of war.

The letter to the *Sunday Telegraph* was not the only interesting later verdict on the Dieppe Raid provided by Reyburn in the post-war years. In the appendix you can also find two articles he wrote in 1980 and 1990 linked to books on the raid that appeared in the *Birmingham Post*, then a leading English regional daily newspaper covering the West Midlands where I was working as a feature writer.

The raid may have been a misconceived operation. But these features showed how Canadian forces, men coming to the aid of Britain of their own free will, parked by England's south-east coast for two years under what seemed far too often like 'a celestial rain cloud', were enthusiastically looking forward to finally getting a shot at the enemy.

The articles also highlighted that the highly regarded German military machine was not flawless as the much-vaunted 10th Panzers headed to Dieppe with 'a speed of advance no better than the rate of a bicycle formation', a neat observation that overlooked the fact that a bike at speed was not that slow.

Neither did Dieppe deprive my father of his sense of humour. Opening his 1980 article praising Ronald Atkin's book *Dieppe 1942: The Jubilee Disaster* (London: Macmillan, 1980), he wrote: 'Having reads a dozen books on the Dieppe Raid including my own ...'

Analysing the disaster that was Dieppe is not that easy a task as shown by the differing takes on the raid by the three major figures seeking an effective Allied attack on the European mainland against the Germans: Lord Mountbatten, General Bernard Montgomery and Prime Minister Winston Churchill.

Regarding themselves as men of destiny, Mountbatten and Montgomery both ensured their reputations were not unduly damaged by the terrible price paid by Canadian troops in the raid. Mountbatten had all the attributes of a natural leader, charisma, charm allied to an unshakeable belief in his own judgment, and ability to inspire those he commanded.

His bravery in combat was unquestioned but his one weakness was lack of judgment that could be equated with recklessness, reflected in the fact a naval officer in the Admiralty nicknamed him the 'master of disaster'.

As a great-grandson of Queen Victoria who attended his christening, Mountbatten's strong royal connections no doubt aided his rise to fame as one of the most influential British figures in the twentieth century. Despite Dieppe, he later headed the recapture of Burma and Singapore as Supreme Allied Commander in the Far East and then as Viceroy of India oversaw the calamitous division of British India into India and Pakistan in 1947. Later he served as First Sea Lord like his father, and finally Chief of Defence Staff.

In terms of misconceived planning, his role in supervising India becoming independent from British rule offered a parallel to Dieppe but with even more disastrous consequences. Originally Mountbatten was in favour of India being given its independence from Britain as one nation, but complex religious divisions produced the ill-conceived two-state solution advocated by the Muslim League. What followed was one of the greatest catastrophes of the twentieth century. The ethnic savagery that erupted between people previously living together in peace produced a death toll estimated at anything from 200,000 to a million while it was calculated at least 10 million refugees sought new homes either side of the newly created border between Hindu-dominated India and the new Islamic state of Pakistan.

While Mountbatten's narrative that Dieppe was an invaluable rehearsal for D-Day deflected criticism, Montgomery avoided censure through voicing his view that the inexperienced Canadians should never have been used in such a dangerous operation while recognizing that reversing their involvement could be counter-productive and damage morale.

'The Dieppe Raid is a good example of an operation which broke all the rules for the successful conduct of battle' was his retrospective verdict on the operation quoted in Volume I of history professor Nigel Hamilton's epic biography, *The Full Monty*, published in 2001 covering the years 1887–1942. But he never actively opposed the raid during the planning stages or tried to persuade Mountbatten to abandon the plan after it was originally cancelled.

The cast list of influential figures responsible for the doomed venture gaining that unstoppable momentum also included a maverick naval officer, Captain John Hughes-Hallett, who echoed Mountbatten's enthusiasm for the raid. Nicknamed 'Hughes-Hitler' for his abrasive nature contrasting with Mountbatten's easy-going charm, he was rewarded with the role of naval commander for the operation itself but failed to dissuade the far more senior Roberts from persisting with further futile attacks on Dieppe's main beach.

Canadian historian Brian Loring Villa in his 1989 book *Unauthorized Action: Mountbatten and the Dieppe Raid 1942* dismissively said of Hughes-Hallett's claim that the raid 'proved once and for all that a frontal assault against a strongly defended port was not on' could 'scarcely impress anyone save complete neophytes in the art of war.'

Interestingly, Churchill's measured verdict on Dieppe in *The Hinge of Fate* was somewhat contradicted after the war when he referred to the relative secrecy involved in deciding to go ahead with Operation

Jubilee that provides the central theme of Brian Loring Villa's book. Nigel Hamilton in his Montgomery biography recalled: 'Eight years after the disaster following a stroke that affected his memory and when writing his history of World War II, he asked: "Surely the decision could not have been taken without the chiefs of staff being informed. If so why did they not bring it to my attention?"'

After Dieppe, Wallace Reyburn followed the Canadian 1st Division fighting the Germans in the Italian campaign, and his experiences as a war correspondent in the latter part of the war also took him to Greece and Yugoslavia.

There was no obvious evidence that he came close again to losing his life as happened so frequently on 19 August 1942 when he scrambled ashore with Canadian troops who paid such a high price for being given the task of testing out those formidable German defences on the French coastline.

In *Some of It Was Fun*, his second book on his Second World War experiences produced by Toronto publishers Thomas Nelson & Sons in 1949, Reyburn looked at the lighter side of the war, where humour helped those fighting the war cope with the trauma of conflict. While the book is of no great interest today as the narrative's cast list largely involved characters he worked alongside whose names mean little to the present generation of Canadians, Reyburn's eye for the telling anecdote did provide some revealing insights that remain relevant today. He found while the Americans and British may have been fighting side by side, they were soldiers with widely differing national characteristics. This was evident when he recalled a classic example of British sangfroid at the Battle of Monte Cassino in which Allied forces fought a bloody encounter from December 1943 until May 1944 against the Axis troops blocking the route to Rome in the town dominated by the mountaintop Benedictine abbey:

When the Allied advance in Italy was held up at Monte Cassino, it was essential that the town was taken. After several attempts by the Americans, a battalion of the British 8th Army was called in. Giving instructions, their commanding officer said that one detachment would approach the left flank and another from the right – 'And we'll rendezvous at the station,' he said. 'Any particular platform, sir?' he was asked.

The book also recounts the most disturbing wartime experience recorded by my father that occurred earlier in the Italian campaign in the town of Bari on 2 December 1943. Recalling a press conference held just outside the southern Italian port by Air Marshal Sir Arthur Coningham, 'a past master at putting his foot in it', he wrote:

> *Said Coningham: 'If a German bomber showed itself over Bari I would regard it as a personal insult.' Five hours later 34 personal insults showed themselves over Bari. But what made this air raid newsworthy wasn't so much the fact it was carried out despite Coningham's very assured pronouncement. It was newsworthy for another reason – a reason so hush-hush that nobody was ever allowed to write about it during the war. All that was ever announced were the bare details that 34 Germans had raided Bari and that over 1,000 people had been killed.*
>
> *Anybody who knew anything about air raids was amazed at those figures., They were quite out of proportion. It seemed impossible that a raid as relatively small as a 34-plane one could cause the deaths of a 1,000 people. Night-long raids on London by hundreds of German planes seldom caused as many as 1,000 casualties, let alone 1,000 deaths.*

Poison gas shells released by the bombing explained the high casualty count and the last thing the Allies wanted was the Germans to discover was this lethal weapon was being stored as a preventative measure. Reyburn's narrative then descended into hearsay, no doubt circulating amongst war correspondents as he mistakenly described the gas stored on the harbour ships as a lethal variety developed by British scientists, and he also claimed an antidote was not dispatched to Bari for fear the Germans would become aware the Allies had large supplies of poison gas.

It was decades before the true story emerged when the German bombers created what was described as 'a little Pearl Harbor' attacking the Allied shipping tightly packed into the ancient harbour. The chemical weapons catastrophe was the result of the casing breaking on mustard gas shells stored on the US Navy Liberty ship *John Harvey*.

The *John Harvey* avoided a direct hit. But such was the carnage caused by the raid that the ship caught fire with disastrous consequences as its lethal cargo of 2,000 mustard gas bombs, each weighing nearly 100 lb, split open and the ship went up in a mushroom cloud, rocking the harbour. Mustard gas mixed with the harbour water proved a lethal combination.

The man who emerged from this sorry episode as a hero was Lieutenant Colonel Stuart Alexander, a physician and cardiologist turned chemical weapons expert, who was sent to the port to lead the American investigation into the disaster.

Despite Churchill's determined denial that chemical weapons were involved, Alexander established beyond doubt the American shells were responsible for the disaster, tracking the *John Harvey* as the source of the chemical weapons.

Allied attempts to cover up the disaster were in vain as an Italian frogman loyal to the Fascists recovered fragments of M47 bomb casing in the harbour that contained the mustard gas, thus confirming the chemical weapons were American.

Besides using his medical expertise aiding the raid casualties, Alexander's impressive report contained the important information that the gas had killed white blood cells, thus paving the way for the future development of chemotherapy as a cancer treatment.

Italy also provided a lethal experience that killed thirty-six civilians that had nothing to do with the war when Reyburn found it was raining gravel from Mount Vesuvius erupting when he was in a jeep approaching the ruined Roman city of Pompeii. Recalling this weird experience in his book, Reyburn wrote:

This was in March 1944 when the mountain had its worst eruption this century. Vesuvius was spewing a column of smoke and dust about twenty thousand feet into the air.

As we approached Pompeii, we found it was raining gravel. We were now directly under the mass of smoke that was roaring up from the crater of the mountain and the roadway was over three foot deep in gravel. Trucks passed us loaded with soldiers and equipment and the men told us they were evacuating. 'Get your tin hats on,' they said. 'This stuff's dangerous. One of our guys got his collarbone broken with a lump the size of a football'.

To bring their point home to us they indicated some tents at the side of the road. There were great gashes in the canvas where pieces of lava, thrown up thousands of feet into the air had come crashing down to earth. A few big lumps thudding around us, one of them missing our jeep by only a few feet, convinced us that we'd better join the evacuation.

As we drove way from Pompeii we were surprised to see that there were few signs of panic among the Italians. We stopped and talked to one man and he merely shrugged his shoulders philosophically. 'Italy is a country built for sorrow,' he said.

Reyburn had previously been to Pompeii before viewing it as a fascinating place, recalling:

You only needed a little imagination to visualize what life had been like in 79 B.C. when the biggest eruption Vesuvius has ever turned on buried the city in cinders. What happened was that the cinders fell to a depth of twenty feet or so but it had been a gradual fall with the result that only the roofs had collapsed from the weight of the cinders and the walls had been left standing. The result was that years later when Pompeii was excavated it was a perfectly preserved example of a Roman city of that day – except there were no roofs. You can stroll through its streets and see the lines of shops, including one that looks exactly like a modern American soda shop. You can also look at the remains of what was obviously a very well equipped brothel.

On the walls of some buildings there are still election slogans painted on the stone facades. In the suburbs you can see you can see the homes of what were Pompeii's well-to-do. On the outskirts of the city you can visit the ball park. And you come away feeling that 2,000 years hasn't brought that much change to the set-up of our cities!

Before heading to Pompeii for the second time, we had read Plini's account of the account of the 79 B.C. eruption. It had been sent out by one of the news agencies as a news report on the present eruption and no readers noticed it as very different from a modern news story until the agency let them in on the secret. Further evidence of the terrific strides we've made in 2,000 years!

Reyburn's experiences as a war correspondent in the eastern European theatre of war later took him to Yugoslavia where with his naturally inquisitive nature he was intrigued when he encountered Russian soldiers, recalling:

I saw a good deal of Russian soldiers while I was in Yugoslavia. I went out of my way to talk to as many as I could – both the Russian men and also the Russian army girls, very smartly uniformed young ladies who wore their fur caps at a jaunty angle.

They'd talk at great length about the 'villis', which they felt was the best American contribution to the war. (They never used the word 'jeep' – villis was their attempt to pronounce the word Willys, which appeared on the back of every jeep by that firm). They'd talk about the Partisans and vodka and the weather. If they took a liking to you they would immediately want to exchange their handkerchief for yours, explaining that this was a custom they had to show friendship. But make one mention of Stalin or life in Russia and that was the end of the conversation. No matter how affable the Russians might feel towards you or he even might be thoroughly in his cups, any question on those lines caused him to shut up immediately. However, I did learn that there were a great shortage of wrist watches in Russia. It wasn't necessary for any Russian to tell me this. Whenever a Russian would see a good watch on someone's wrist he would automatically buy it or take it away from him – depending on the status of the watch-owner. How notorious they were for watch-snatching was borne out one afternoon when I was watching a newsreel at a movie house in Belgrade. The newsreel showed Churchill welcoming Stalin as he descended from a transport plane. Churchill was wearing a watch-chain across his ample waistline and as Stalin came forward with his hand in front of him in greeting the voice of a child in the audience piped up: 'There goes his watch!'

Reyburn was one of a small group of war correspondents in Belgrade in February 1945 when the British Field Marshal Alexander came to meet Marshal Tito. The event resulted in the Canadian war correspondent finding himself engaged in a remarkable one-to-one conversation with the charismatic Partisan leader engaged in driving the Germans out of Yugoslavia, who was later hailed as one of the twentieth century's great soldier statesmen.

Alexander regularly had tea with the war correspondents during his stay and while revealing no details of the military aspects of his talks with Tito, he wasn't in the least bit reluctant to voice the fact he was impressed with the man he had come to see in Belgrade.

Reyburn recalled Alexander saying: 'I liked Tito from our first meeting. He's a sincere man you can deal with honestly and straight-forwardly as he puts his cards on the table.' And he himself was to see Tito, immaculately turned out in his full-dress grey marshal's uniform with its red patches with gold braid leaves on his tunic lapels, several times, but only after penetrating the elaborate system of guards which surrounded him wherever he went.

'He is well built and when I first met him, I approached him from the back,' wrote Reyburn in *Some of It Was Fun*. 'His broad shoulders and slim waist struck me as the sort of thing you see in body-building advertisements. However, in front there is a suggestion of fullness, which has come along with his fifty-nine years.

'He has a strong face with kindly eyes and a warm smile. He is amiable and quietly-spoken. He has a confident and assured manner and a great deal of charm about him.'

The night before Alexander left Belgrade, Tito held a reception in the city's royal palace where the Partisan leader went to the trouble of welcoming each guest personally while by his side was his German shepherd dog, Tiger. It was a greeting easily remembered as Reyburn recalled:

Considering the splendour of the surroundings and the fact that every high ranking British, American and Russian officer and government official within hailing distant was present, it was a paradise for stuffed shirts. Tito, however, acted just like any ordinary person giving a party in his own home. He's very fond of his dog and as the guests arrived he showed them proudly how intelligent Tiger was. He got him to 'play dead', roll over, beg and do his other tricks and he got a big kick when Tiger came through with a faultless performance.

Tito's conviviality was by no means short-lived. Going from guest to guest ensuring they were 'getting enough to eat,' he was later joining the sing-song when the entertainers at the function broke into Partisan marching songs.

My father always amused us recalling how when he was about to leave the party, Tito told him: 'Don't go now Wally.' This didn't appear in print but he did write that Tito was unhappy at the suggestion anybody should leave, telling his guests: 'Things are just starting to warm up, don't leave now.'

When Reyburn did decide around four o'clock it really was time to depart, he sought out his host to say goodbye, finally tracking him down to the palace library where he was alone, chewing a pork chop from a plate of food from the buffet, explaining with a broad smile: 'I felt it was about time I had something to eat.' What followed was a remarkably revealing conversation as Tito detailed in good, if slightly haltingly English, his political philosophy. He explained the rift that existed in his country between the Croatians in the north and the Serbs in the south in terms of not only religion but also outlook and background.

'Before the war Yugoslavia was ruled from Belgrade,' he told the war correspondent, offering an insight into the state of his country. 'The king would never move out of this part of the country, never go to

Croatia.' Behind the king were the Serbian hegemonists – the diehard Serbs who regarded Yugoslavia as Greater Serbia.

'These people are among my chief enemies in the country at present. They don't like the idea of uniting all the different races in Yugoslavia in one federation, each with equal rights.'

Tito also explained that Yugoslavia was dominated by Russia in the same way Canada was dominated by the United States, but the final court of appeal was within 'our own country. We make our own laws here, they aren't made in Moscow for us'. Prophetically, Reyburn foresaw Yugoslavia run by Tito after the war ended, writing:

I came away from Yugoslavia feeling that the people of the country, so accustomed over the years to authoritarian rule, haven't an inkling of democracy as we know it. All they seem to understand is dictatorship and the best they could ever hope for was a benign dictatorship. The type of dictatorship Tito planned to give the Yugoslavs, judged on what I saw of its workings, seemed infinitely better than the Royalist dictatorship under which the Yugoslavs had suffered before the war.

My father's experiences in the later war years never matched the drama of Dieppe, which tellingly rated no mention in his account of the lighter side of the war. His role following troops in the Eastern Europe theatre meant he didn't cover the D-Day landings that ultimately brought down Hitler. However, the events he recollected were far from insignificant.

The 1944 Vesuvius eruption was a major natural disaster and his description of the appeal of the ruins of Pompeii could easily have been translated into a compelling advert for the benefit of the post-war Italian tourist board.

His analysis of the character of the Russian troops refusing to pass comment on Stalin had echoes in the early decades of the twenty-first century, with Vladimir Putin ruthlessly dealing with opponents daring to question his leadership.

Tito's vision of a united Yugoslavia under his control outlined in the White Palace library in Belgrade in the final year of the war to the young Canadian war correspondent indeed came to pass. But after his death in 1980, the potential powder keg Tito had kept under control was to explode, alarming the western world.

Although Tito had outlined the sharply conflicting interests in his country during their conversation, Reyburn could hardly have envisaged that nearly fifty years later Canadian troops would be serving in the Balkans as part of the United Nations peacekeeping mission in the early 1990s; and that Yugoslavia was to disappear, resurfacing as a spate of new countries, Serbia and Montenegro, Macedonia, Bosnia-Herzegovina and Croatia.

Although he was a war correspondent with the Canadian Army, Wallace Reyburn was in fact born in Auckland, New Zealand in 1913 where his father was a leading dentist.

His travels began at an early age. His family were originally Scottish immigrants and his generation of New Zealanders always referred to the UK as 'home'. Somewhat bizarrely, a chance encounter with an English family on an Auckland beach led to young Reyburn being sent to England as a boarder to complete his education at Berkhamsted School in Hertfordshire, where the novelist Graham Greene's father was headmaster. Talking to the English family, Reyburn's mother, Florence, had been very impressed with the behaviour of their young boy and asked where he went to school. So, they later decided their son should also be educated there.

When his schooldays finished, he studied at Auckland University but never completed his degree course, instead becoming a journalist. He returned to Europe covering the 1935/6 All Blacks rugby tour for the *New Zealand Herald* and remained north of the equator for the rest of his life.

By the time the Second World War broke out, Reyburn's appetite for travel had taken him to Canada where he was working for the McLean Publishing Company's *Chatelaine* magazine in Toronto. It was then he met his first wife, Lucille Mae Peart, who was fashion editor of *Mayfair*, another McLean magazine.

When they married, the woman he simply referred to as 'Lucille' in his book embarked on a somewhat unexpected career change. Describing their marriage in *Some of It Was Fun*, he advised:

Never marry a spy. I did – and I advise against it. Of course I married the right sort of spy (she was on our side) but I never got to see her. In the four years we were married I saw her for a total of about eight days. She was always off on some mysterious junket, precisely where, I was never allowed to know, I'd say there is only one route to happiness when married to a spy – divorce.

They were only married a couple of days before my father left for overseas as a war correspondent in February 1941. It wasn't until after the Dieppe Raid he returned home to Canada.

'She was overjoyed to have her husband home safe and sound, even it was for a short time,' wrote my father. 'Two days later she disappeared. Just like that. Not even as much as "This is going to tough for both of us." I just woke up one morning to find her not around. All her belongings gone, not a trace of her.'

A few days later a letter arrived cryptically announcing her new address from then on would be 'Care of Postmaster, New York, N.Y.' There would be no point in contacting her and that he should just use her maiden name.

Further letters he sent received no reply. But, by an extraordinary coincidence they did meet again before the Italian campaign as my father recalled:

Walking down the main street of Tunis one day, whom should I bump into but the Poor Man's Mata Hari. I was very pleased to see her but she looked at me the way you look at a fellow to whom you have just fondly said farewell and he comes back to say he missed his train. Encountering me was obviously very bothersome to her. It meant complications.

The interview was very short. She explained she had to wipe the marriage from her mind – just as if it hadn't happened. She was now on paper a single person, engaged in certain work. 'Please don't embarrass me by trying to see me anymore,' she said.

So that was that. I didn't see her again during the war, haven't seen her since. She didn't even show up for the divorce.

Back in the real world after the war ended, Reyburn, who acquired both Canadian citizenship and a place in Canada's *Who's Who* for his war reporting, became editor of *New Liberty* magazine in Toronto, where I was born in 1946.

His friends included the Canadian novelist Scott Young, whose first name was given to my younger brother. In later years, my mother enjoyed surprising people by relating how she used to babysit the younger son of the writer, who later found worldwide fame as the singer/songwriter Neil Young.

In 1950, Wallace Reyburn moved to England to take up a post as the London columnist for the *Toronto Telegram*. He was to remain in the capital for the rest of his life where in his career as a writer he produced twenty-five books. These covered a wide range of topics. His best-selling *Flushed with Pride: The Life and Times of Thomas Crapper*, first published in England by Macdonald & Co. in 1969, followed by American publishers Prentice-Hall in 1971, was described as being deftly pitched between 'the informative and the tongue in cheek' and attracted criticism for over-praising the Victorian master plumber as the perfector of the flushed lavatory. Some even dismissed the book as a hoax, however Crapper's firm survives today based in Huddersfield, Yorkshire selling Victorian-style sanitaryware.

What was a complete hoax was his later book published in 1972 titled *Bust-up: The Uplifting Tale of Otto Titzling and the Development of the Bra*. But this failed to prevent Titzling being mistaken as a real person as the inventor of the bra.

In 1994, Canadian journalist Chris Haney, co-inventor of Trivial Pursuit, listed 'What did Otto Titzling invent?' as his favourite question in the board game that sold more than a million copies while six years earlier Bette Midler could be found singing a song titled 'Otto Titzling' in the 1988 movie *Beaches*.

On a more serious level, Reyburn wrote the first biography of the celebrated British satirist and broadcaster Sir David Frost titled *Frost: Anatomy of a Success* (1968) as well as an acclaimed candid portrait of the popular British radio personality and wit Gilbert Harding hailed as 'the rudest man in Britain' published in 1978.

Reyburn's father had been honorary dental surgeon to the Auckland Rugby Union, enabling his son easy access to Eden Park, the spiritual home of New Zealand rugby where Test cricket was also played, enabling Reyburn to witness England's Wally Hammond set a new Test record, scoring 336 not out versus New Zealand in April 1933.

His devotion to rugby union not only brought him north of the equator in 1935: in the 1960s and 1970s, he produced nine rugby books including the first history of the legendary British Lions rugby tour, a history of the England rugby team and Twickenham, regarded as the HQ of the sport. *The Unsmiling Giants*, his book covering the celebrated 1967 All Blacks tour of Britain, was hailed as 'a minor miracle as sports books go' by *Punch* magazine.

However, his ambition to become a successful novelist never came to pass. He greatly admired Somerset Maugham (1874–1965), a major English literary figure in his day celebrated for his novels, plays and mastery of the short story. In many ways his own writing matched the unadorned clarity of Maugham's prose and shrewd understanding of human nature.

Unlike Maugham, Reyburn found his five published novels attracted no reviews and suffered poor sales. But he retained his sense of humour. *The Street That Died* published by Cassell in 1960 echoed his own happy experiences as a young New Zealander living in London in the late 1930s and then returning from Canada to a very different city in the post-war years with the road where he had lived before the war wrecked by bomb damage. Inside the cover of a signed copy he had given to a friend I came across in a second-hand bookshop in the Welsh border town of Hay-on-Wye, he wrote: 'At last! A copy of *The Book That Died!*'

Known as 'Wally' rather than 'Wallace', my father was not the easiest man to live with and his more extreme views highlighted by his fondness for controversial generalizations would have been derided by many in the Britain of the twenty-first century. If the Feminist Movement had been into book burning, doubtless *The Inferior Sex*, his detailed account of how men outperformed women in every field, ranging from cooking and fashion to literature and politics and published by Prentice Hall in 1972, would be top of the hit list.

My father's belief that the Conservatives were the only party fit to rule the UK briefly surfaced when he compared the Dieppe Raid to a socialist venture – 'fine in theory but unworkable in practice.'

The fact Labour prime minister Clement Attlee in the post-war years arguably provided Britain's greatest peacetime government and the National Health Service, which served my father so well in his final years when ill-health became a problem, never quite registered.

I recall it being beyond his understanding the fact I voted Labour in a local Greater London Council election as they opposed an environmentally damaging road scheme scheduled to pass through the attractive residential environs of north-west London.

His other shortcoming included a stubborn failure to realize that home ownership was a major feature of British life. 'Always rent' was his philosophy after the home he had bought in Port Credit on the north shore of Lake Ontario dropped in value as it became surrounded by a new development when he came to sell it on his move to England.

The result was that despite earning what was a very high salary by UK post-war standards working for the *Toronto Telegram,* he ended up spending years unwisely paying a huge rent for an attractive mid-nineteenth-century stucco Victorian villa in one of the most desirable roads in St John's Wood leading down to Lord's Cricket Ground where the home of Brian Johnston, the hugely popular broadcaster and cricket commentator, could be found.

After our family later moved to a more modest two-floor garden flat in the Hampstead area, hordes of mini-skirted girls could be found perched on the front wall of the our former home waiting for a sighting of Beatle Paul McCartney, who had bought the house facing ours on the other side of the road. In 2020, the home where I spent my younger years playing numerous games of cricket and croquet in the back garden with my father had an estimated value of just over £9 million (more than 15 million Canadian dollars).

My father's more extreme views and fondness for generalizations tended to be sidelined in public where he hugely enjoyed engaging in convivial conversations with people he was meeting for the first time in a pub or at social gatherings, invariably amusing those he encountered with his smiling trademark farewell remark: 'Nice talking to you. Keep in touch!'

Nevertheless, he also had the ability to end a conversation with a cutting remark when he thought it was justified. Visiting his local pub in St John's Wood with him in 1968, we found a rather brash American loudly informing everyone how his country's military were doing the free world a service fighting the spread of Communism. This was the year the North Koreans held the crew of USS *Pueblo* hostage for eleven months after capturing the American naval vessel, claiming it was a spyship.

The American was finally silenced when he found those around him laughing after my father asked him: 'By the way, have you got your boat back yet?' His favourite trivia question invariably left people perplexed. Asked 'Who was born as a result of the Immaculate Conception?', people found it hard to comprehend the answer wasn't 'Jesus Christ'. But look in any dictionary and you will find the answer is the 'doctrine that the Virgin Mary was conceived free from the taint of original sin'. In 1854, this had been declared an article of faith of the Roman Catholic Church. Christ was in fact the Virgin Birth as the Christian doctrine held that Jesus was conceived by his mother Mary through the power of the Holy Spirit. Perhaps the Immaculate Conception should have been rephrased as the 'Immaculate Misconception'.

My father's ability to engage with complete strangers and putting them instantly at ease never deserted him. Near the end of his life, he had people in a crowded hospital lift laughing after he and I squeezed in just before the doors shut. Facing everyone already in the lift, he looked at those crammed in front of us and then announced: 'I suppose you are all wondering why I have asked you all to attend this meeting?'

By contrast, our mother was a selfless character with an equally strong personality, well able to hold her own in any marital argument and she never lost her strong Canadian accent despite spending most of her life in London.

Puzzlingly, she was pictured, notebook in hand, alongside Ces Merritt VC, at the press conference held after his wartime imprisonment, at Crookham, England on 21 April 1945. Listed as representing Thomson Newspapers, presumably her brother Ross Munro had arranged this assignment, arguing it was worth getting a woman's view on what it was like encountering a Canadian war hero.

This unlikely event matched the enterprising side of her character. After I, my sister and younger brother had grown up and left home, she embarked on a successful career in the London magazine world with no previous experience that we were aware of. Perhaps it was just as well that the names she gave as references from magazines the other side of the Atlantic were not checked as they were all dead.

She held her own spending many happy years serving as deputy editor of *Woman's Journal,* one of the longest-running UK women's magazines before it closure in 2001. A great admirer of the American writer F. Scott Fitzgerald, she had the happy task of commissioning the literary content of this well-designed magazine well known for its fiction extracts.

After her death in 1996, the past loomed larger in my father's life and in his final years he told me he found he was experiencing nightmares, remembering the day he came close to losing his life on several occasions.

Literary interest in the raid continued into the twenty-first century and 2020 saw the publication of Patrick Bishop's superbly written *Operation Jubilee – Dieppe 1942: The Folly and the Sacrifice,* while American Leah Garrett in her book, X-*Troop: The Secret Jewish Commandos of World Two,* offered new evidence of a secret mission to steal the latest Enigma machine developed by the Germans and housed in Dieppe by taking advantage of the attack on the town.

A small group of German refugee soldiers who had fled from Nazi-annexed Sudetenland were trained for the task. Garrett disclosed a long-classified report by one of the soldiers, known as Maurice Latimer by his anglicized name, revealed orders 'to proceed immediately to the German HQ in Dieppe to pick up all documents, etc of value, including, if possible, a new German respirator [Enigma code machine].'

The raid was a failure and troops never gained control of town; only Latimer was able to return to England unscathed as one of his fellow soldiers was killed, another badly injured and two were captured, spending the rest of the war in German hard labour camps.

However, claiming this cloak-and-dagger mission was a prime aim of the raid was to say the least far-fetched. Did it really make sense endangering the lives of more than 6,000 troops in the largest amphibious operation since Gallipoli?

Interestingly, Mountbatten in the post-war years never publicly cited the Enigma mission as a major factor in the Dieppe plan. This is odd considering the great lengths he went to in justifying the disaster. As Bishop wryly noted in his book: 'He made the case so often that it sometimes seemed that the main person he was trying to convince was himself.'

If Latimer and his companions had succeeded in getting into the Hotel Moderne in Dieppe where the intelligence operation was housed, would not the Germans have developed a new version of the Enigma machine realizing it might well have been compromised during the raid? The real Allied triumph discovering German plans was provided by the genius of Alan Turing and other staff at Bletchley Park, giving the Allies a golden opportunity to counter enemy military activities without him realizing encrypted messages had been deciphered in a Buckinghamshire country house.

One of the post-war oddities was that among the extensive list of authoritative books on the raid, my father's account remained forgotten until after its third edition was published in 1958.

While Wallace Reyburn as a war correspondent didn't match the prose mastery of Ernest Hemingway or the intellect of Martha Gellhorn, he was a gifted storyteller with a journalist's instinct for the revealing anecdote allied with a sense of humour that offered a drama-ridden, invaluable first-hand insight into the reality facing the Canadians troops sent on a doomed mission at Dieppe. Unlike the authors of the many post-war books on the raid, Reyburn was actually at Dieppe.

However, my father never told me he felt his account of the raid should remain in print. Possibly this was because it was written under wartime conditions and he was unhappy it backed Mountbatten's narrative.

But he did hold the view it was odd the raid was never the subject of a major film when so many Second World War battles were. To those who argue defeats were not film material, he pointed out this didn't prevent the Charge of the Light Brigade and Dunkirk being screened.

His book can be divided into two parts. Explaining why Dieppe was raided, he provides an impressively detailed justification for the operation that matches the Mountbatten and Combined Operation Headquarters viewpoint he contradicted in the post-war years free from the burden of censorship and propaganda.

Then came his vivid blow-by-blow account of his own experiences in the raid, showing why sending 6,000 troops into battle against a well-defended Channel port was a flawed plan with no chance of success.

Forget the first part of the book and you have a dramatic, drama-ridden account of the reality of warfare, laden with astute observations as well as brief conversations with those fighting at Dieppe offering an insight into their mindset when confronted by danger and a formidable enemy.

It is a book that deserves to remain in print if only to preserve the memory of a brave generation of young Canadians, many of whom lost their lives fighting a just cause.

Wallace Reyburn was involved in the least disastrous of the three Dieppe Raid beach attacks. At Pourville before dawn broke, the South Saskatchewan Regiment were the only troops to scramble ashore avoiding enemy fire.

In the street battles that followed, the buildings in the small resort the other side of Dieppe town's western headland offered some welcome cover. However the 523 SSRs who embarked faced an impossible task against superior firepower. They never reached intended targets at Quatre Vents Farm and the radar station further inland nor prevented the Queen's Own Cameron Highlanders (Camerons) being hit with enemy fire when they later landed at Pourville.

While the withdrawal on Pourville's beach proved a traumatic experience, the carnage elsewhere was on a different scale. The doomed Royals attack on Puys beach the eastern side of Dieppe resulted in 227 deaths, 264 prisoners of war and just 65 (including 33 wounded) members of the battalion making it back to England.

On Dieppe's huge main beach, the assault aimed at capturing the town proved a costly failure after the preliminary air attack and destroyers offshore lacked the firepower to inflict any significant damage on the powerful German defences.

The Royal Hamilton Light Infantry (nicknamed The Rileys) did manage to capture the casino. But the small groups of soldiers who managed to get into the town could inflict only limited damage. Taking the town and further inland targeting the St-Aubin airfield proved unattainable.

Fifteen of the twenty-seven Churchill tanks ashore negotiated the awkward pebble beach to reach the promenade directing their firepower at enemy positions. But the engineers casualty count in the landing meant the road blocks preventing their entry into the town remained intact.

Unlike Pourville, troops were pinned to Dieppe's long main beach for hours on end with just the air battle and smokescreens hindering enemy fire. While the SSRs in Pourville lost 84 men, The Rileys (197), Essex Scottish (121) and Les Fusiliers (119) Dieppe paid a far higher price for failure in the main attack.

The catalogue of problems in the raid seemed never ending ranging from the navigational difficulties crossing the Channel on time at night, the Focke-Wulfe 190s holding sway over the Spitfire Mark Vs in the air battle, untested Sten guns jamming and an error prone wireless communications system failing to convey the true situation ashore as well as resulting in some landing craft that could have evacuated men in the withdrawal heading home prematurely.

The Dieppe Raid was effectively backed by a formidable array of leading military commanders: Mountbatten, Montgomery, the Canadian corps commander Lieutenant General Harry Crerar, the RAF Air Vice-Marshal Trafford Leigh-Mallory and also Churchill himself. Analysing the many, often contradictory, judgments on the raid, the inevitable conclusion is Dieppe provided a classic example of expertise tragically overriding common sense.

The raid was also a dramatic reminder of the reality of traditional warfare involving troops in direct combat with each other. Just three years later as the Second World War drew to a close, the Americans showed how countless thousands could be killed and vast tracts of land destroyed without deploying armies when they dropped atomic bombs on the Japanese cities of Hiroshima and Nagasaki.

This horrifying evidence of science's ability to dehumanise warfare was summed up by J. Robert Oppenheimer, head of The Manhatten Project that created the atomic bomb, reciting the apocalyptic quote from Hindu scripture: 'I am become death, the destroyer of worlds.'

Whatever scars Dieppe left on his psyche, Wallace Reyburn never wavered in his lifelong, unqualified admiration for the Royal Navy, who lost seventy-five men in the raid. Although the raid was masterminded by a naval commander, he wouldn't countenance any criticism of the service that had enabled him to escape from the carnage of a doomed military mission.

No doubt, as his mind inevitably dwelt on flashbacks in his Belsize Park garden flat in north-west London as his life neared its close in the summer of 2001, the memory of witnessing the inspirational bravery of Lieutenant Colonel Ces Merritt, Canada's first VC of the Second World War, on that bridge at Pourville, was not forgotten.

Ross Reyburn
Moseley, Birmingham,
England, 2022

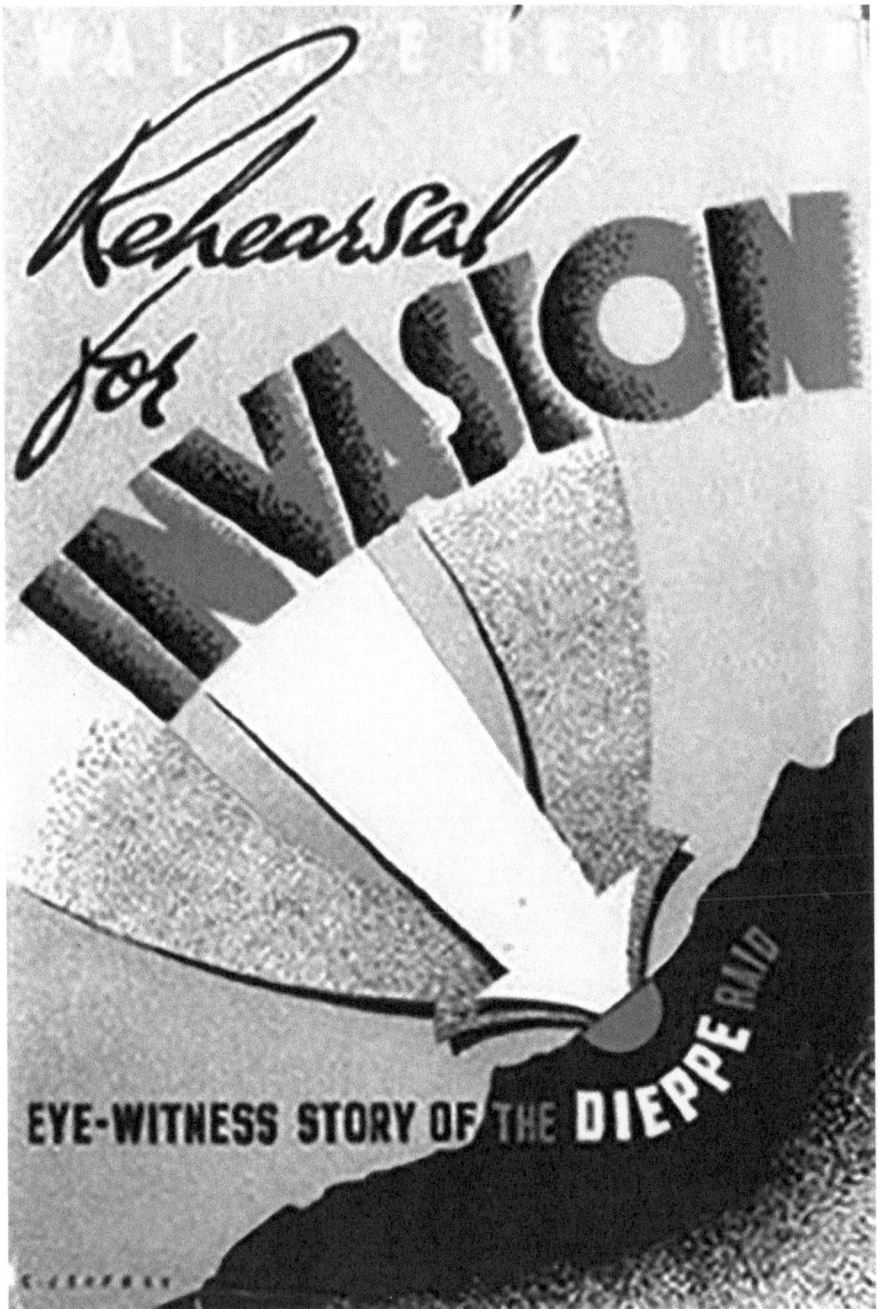

Cover of the first edition of Wallace Reyburn's eyewitness account of the Dieppe Raid, *Rehearsal for Invasion*, published by George G. Harrap & Co Ltd. in 1943.

PART TWO

Rehearsal for Invasion

Eye-Witness Story of the Dieppe Raid

Wallace Reyburn OBE

Published in 1943 by George Harrap & Co., this is a reprint of the first edition of Canadian war correspondent Wallace Reyburn's account of the Dieppe Raid that took place on 19 August 1942.

Chapter 1

Why Dieppe was Raided

I

In the early part of August 1942 I attended a Second Front rally in Trafalgar Square. The place was jam-packed with people. They stood in thousands listening to the speakers assembled at the base of Nelson's Column and shouting their views at microphones which relayed their demands for a Second Front over a public address system until every corner of London S.W.1. seemed to ring with their voices.

There was another Second Front meeting taking place on the same Sunday afternoon at the Hippodrome Theatre, a little way up Charing Cross Road from Trafalgar Square.

It was a season of Second Front rallies, that early part of 1942's summer. Nobody in Britain was pleased about the way the war was going. Hong Kong and then Singapore had fallen. Things were going badly for us in the Middle East. In Russia Soviet troops were fighting with their backs to the wall, fending off the onslaught of the Germans. The enemy had reached the gates of Stalingrad. Churchill had hied to Moscow and was conferring with Stalin.

There was an increasing demand by the people of Britain, echoed by the Press and public in America, for effective action by the Allies, an end to our long succession of withdrawals. There was a feeling something must be done to help Russia.

A current story was going the rounds about a man looking up from his newspaper in a railway carriage and saying, 'We aren't doing too badly,' to receive a curt rejoinder from the man opposite him: 'For a Russian you speak very good English.'

People felt, and many expressed the view at great length in the public prints and from soap-boxes, that for their part the Russians were doing a terrific job in eastern Europe, but when were we going to open up a front in the west to supplement their efforts?

Most ardent of these agitators for offensive action on our part were the men of the Canadian Army Overseas. They did not give voice to their impatience from platforms, save for one or two bold enough to ignore the Army regulation against soldiers taking part in public meetings. But inside them was a burning desire to 'get going' and it found expression in their talk among themselves at their camps and in conversation with other Forces and civilians in pubs when they were on leave. They frequently broke loose and raised some mild hell, which brought on them the severe criticism of some English people who didn't go to the trouble of thinking the thing through and realizing that the Canadians' hell-raising was not, as they thought, a product of hooliganism, but was directly traceable to the fact that the men from the Dominion had joined up on their own free will to have a crack at the enemy, and had spent over two years stationed in Britain, and as yet had not come to grips with the Jerries.

The first contingent of Canadians arrived in Britain in December 1939. Since then convoy after convoy of them had poured across the Atlantic, until the total had risen to a hundred and fifty thousand. They were all volunteers. At first, with the prospect of a German invasion of the country imminent, their task was primarily a defensive one. They were allocated a sector of Britain to defend, and their training was directed towards repelling the enemy if and when he stepped on to these shores.

But the months went by and the likelihood of invasion lessened, the accent of their training was switched from defence to offence. They were trained as shock troops. Their chief, Lieutenant-General McNaughton, announced that the Canadian Army 'was a dagger pointed at the heart of Berlin.' His men said, 'Okay, let's go,' but 1940 had gone by, 1941 dragged by, and still none of them had tangled with the enemy. Some of them spent eight days in France after Dunkirk on a junket which took them inland and out again via Brest without their getting as much as a sight of the enemy. Another batch of them had gone on a raid to Spitsbergen, up in the Arctic Circle, but they put the wireless and weather-recording installations there out of action without encountering any opposition. These were but minor diversions in a long succession of months and months of training waiting for a real scrap.

They strained at the leash in their camps on the southern downs of England. The English climate, the damp, rainy winters, got on their nerves. They got to feeling the country was under a celestial water-cart. They read with envy the accounts in papers of Australian, New Zealand and other Dominion troops in action.

They fought out their countless mock battles and trudged all over the countryside on endless manoeuvres. In one thing alone they consoled themselves. Soon, surely, they'd go into action; soon something must happen.

Something did happen – Dieppe.

II

There had been previous raids on the Channel coastline of Europe, but never one as big as the Dieppe raid of August 19, 1942.

Dieppe was a Combined Operations raid in daylight, involving land, sea and air forces. It was the prelude, the curtain-raiser, to the North African campaign which was to open three months later. It was the pivot of the Allies' switch-round from the defensive to the offensive in western Europe.

It was not a Commando raid, as its forerunners had been, although some Commando units did take part. It was primarily a landing of infantry and tanks, a reconnaissance in force.

Combined Operations, which was the official title of the section of the British war mechanism that has Lord Louis Mountbatten as its chief and which plans and carries out operations in which the three services combine, has launched a great number of raids on the enemy-occupied coastline. Many of them have been small affairs, perhaps with only a handful of Commandos taking part; others are large in scope. But up to the time of Dieppe, only four of the stabs made at the French coast had been made public.

On the night of February 28, 1942, a force of paratroops came down at Bruneval. They captured the village and destroyed a German wireless station. Their withdrawal was covered by fire from assault craft.

On March 27 the Commandos raided Saint-Nazaire. The destroyer *Campbeltown*, loaded with explosives, was rammed into the lock gate at the outer entrance to the docks and submarine base. The gate was blown away, and Commandos on shore demolished the power-station and destroyed the machinery which operated the inner lock gate. Thus the basin was made tidal and rendered useless to the enemy for some considerable time.

Boulogne was raided on the night of April 21 and again on June 6. These were both reconnaissance raids.

Those four raids and the numerous others about which nothing was published are all carried out by specialist troops. The Commandos and paratroops who took part in them are drawn from units specially trained in demolition work, intelligence, and reconnaissance, and for quick, decisive action against strong-points, batteries etc. But the Dieppe venture, as well as being a much larger proposition, was of quite a different nature. We landed a force of six battalions of infantry of the line, with tanks and ancillary troops, supported by strong air cover, and, strictly speaking, it was more of an invasion rehearsal than a raid. We attacked Dieppe in daylight, not under the cover of darkness as the Commandos usually work, and made flank and frontal assaults on the town. It was the first time in history that it had ever been attempted to land tanks on beaches in the face of enemy opposition.

There were four main objects of the attack. First, we wanted to test the enemy defences on the northern coast of France. Secondly, we wanted to test our ability to land a large military force and tanks on enemy-occupied beaches. Thirdly, we sought to find out by direct combat in the air just what strength the Luftwaffe had in western Europe. And, fourthly, we hoped to demolish wireless stations, anti-aircraft batteries, and the like in the Dieppe area and inflict as much damage to enemy forces and installations as possible.

The last mentioned fact, though it fully occupied the land forces throughout the time they were ashore, was actually the least important object of the raid. There are many things which happen in this war that puzzle us, the general public. We are often quick to criticize those whose job it is to conduct the war on our behalf. After the news of some large-scale operation hits the headlines we armchair military experts are apt to hastily ejaculate, 'Why the hell did they go and do that? It was crazy.' That's what many said immediately after Dieppe. Why, it was asked, was it necessary to land six thousand men to destroy a few ack-ack and shore batteries and wireless stations? Surely, the critics, argue, that could have been done every bit as effectively and without anything like the casualties by one or two well-worked-out, small-scale Commando raids.

In the case of Dieppe, as on other occasions, we rushed to condemn the powers-that-be and omitted to give them credit for having bigger fish to fry. We forgot to fit Dieppe into the broader picture of our war strategy. And the men at the top are in the unfortunate position that they have to take all the criticism without being able to answer it. Usually they can't give the full reason why a certain undertaking was launched without thus disclosing to the enemy future moves they have in mind.

We can see now, though, what Dieppe was all about. General Eisenhower, Commander-in-Chief of our forces in North Africa, sent a cable to Lord Louis Mountbatten after the landings were made in Algiers, Oran, and Casablanca in November. He thanked him for the invaluable help Combined Operations had given him in ensuring that the vast body of American and British troops were effectively got ashore, and stressed the importance of the experience and tactical information gained at Dieppe.

As well as providing much-needed experience of landing troops and heavy fighting vehicles on hostile shores, Dieppe's place in the broad pattern of our offensive strategy in western Europe can now clearly be seen. In the months before, Hitler must have chewed many a carpet trying to figure out where Britain and the United State were going to strike. He knew they'd surely strike soon. But exactly where? – that was the question. The Russian campaign has placed limitations on his strength in the west of land forces, weapons, and equipment, and of air power. How best to deploy what he has at his disposal, to be prepared to faces the Allies wherever they might launch an offensive?

The Dieppe raid was a thrust at his defences on the Channel coastline. The Allies proved to their satisfaction and to Hitler's chagrin that they could land a large force with tanks in that area. It assured the enemy would be kept very much on the *qui vive* along that coast. Then the Allies struck in French North Africa. Thus the Germans, faced with the threat of attack by way of the underside of Europe, were confronted with the assignment of not only having to rush troops and planes to face the Allies in North Africa and prepare for developments on the mainland of southern Europe, but also having to keep their defences in the north as strong as possible, to be on the guard against more and bigger Dieppes, followed by an invasion.

Chapter 2

The Planning and Special Training

I

Why was Dieppe chosen as the locale for the raid?

This port and seaside resort – about twenty-five thousand people lived there normally – is one of the most strongly fortified parts of the coast. Many have wondered why, knowing that we'd get such a hot reception if we went in there, we didn't go ashore at some less formidable spot.

Well, the parts of the north coast of France at which it is feasible to land large numbers of troops and equipment are limited. Much of the coastline consists of steep cliffs, broken only here and there by narrow ravines. Though these steep-sided gullies present little or no problem to small detachments of Commandos, they're dead against the movement of large bodies of troops. Certain points there are, however, where there are flat beaches on the shoreline, ideal for putting ashore an invading force – places like Dieppe, Brest, Dunkirk, and so on. At these points there are also docks, wharves, installations for handling cargoes, which can be used for unloading equipment and stores once the place is taken.

It's safe to surmise that in planning these defences in western Europe the Germans considered the regions at which we would be most likely to launch an invasion would be places like Dieppe, which not only provided good landing beaches and port facilities but are also within fighter range (about a hundred and fifty miles) of Britain's airfields.

Hence the sector between Brest and Ostend may be reckoned as the most heavily fortified part of the coastline. We could probably have landed the same force as that used at Dieppe somewhere else along the coast, down in the Bay of Biscay, say, without encountering such stiff opposition. But that wouldn't have taught us many of the things we wanted to find out.

We wanted to test the defences in the sector in which it was most likely our invasion activities would take place. If we'd gone into Europe without Dieppe we'd have been like the boxer who rushes out of his corner and takes a wild slug at an opponent without sizing him up with some sparring.

II

The first indication I got of how the raid was going to be carried out was on the day we war correspondents headed for the south coast of England to board the ships that would take us across the Channel.

As far as the land forces were concerned, it was to be virtually a Canadian show. Five of the six thousand men put ashore were to be troops drawn from the Second Canadian Division Overseas.

This was the plan.

The transport ships, tank-landing craft, and escort vessels were to set out at night from more than one south of England port. They were to converge on Dieppe, and at 4.50 A.M., at dawn, the first landings were to take place. We were to attack an eleven-mile front.

Five miles along the coast to the west of Dieppe, on our right flank, is a place called Varengeville. Six miles to the east of Dieppe is Berneval. At each of these points the Germans had batteries of six heavy guns. They were coastal defence batteries, guarding the approaches by sea to Dieppe.

At the zero hour the No. 4 Commando unit was to land at Varengeville, take the garrison by surprise, spike their guns, and blow up the ammunition. At the same time, No. 3 Commando would land at Berneval and carry out a similar task. These two assignments were among the most important of the raid, because unless these two batteries were put out of action the flotilla of ships bringing the main forces for the flank and frontal attacks on Dieppe itself would have been put at the mercy of these guns. The Commandos were to depart as soon as they had carried out this part of the operation.

At the precise moment the landing craft touched shore the Commando landings were to be made on each side of Dieppe proper. About a mile along the coast road to the east of the town was a narrow valley leading up from the beach to the town of Puys (our left flank). The Royal Regiment of Canada was to land there and put out of action the forts and pill-boxes high up on the cliffs that would have menaced our troops landing on the main beach at Dieppe. A mile and a half to the west (our right flank) was Pourville beach. Here the South Saskatchewan Regiment was to go ashore, take the town, form a bridgehead across the wide valley behind it, and solidify each side of the valley. Half an hour later, at 5.20, the Cameron Highlanders of Winnipeg were to land at the same beach and advance through this bridgehead made by the South Saskatchewan Regiment.

Then the defence posts situated on the main front, along the beach before Dieppe, were to be subjected to a bombardment by naval guns and Hurricane bombers. This was a softening-up process preparatory to the landing of the infantry and tanks. The Canadian Essex Scottish were to go in on the eastern section of the beach, and simultaneously the Hamilton Light Infantry at the other end.

The Dieppe beach, which is about a mile long, has a sea-wall along its entire length. The wall is about four foot high, and above it is an esplanade, with lawns and pathways, similar to those to be found at many seaside resorts on the English coast. This park separates the beach itself from the hotels and other buildings at the front. At the western end is a casino. This was known to be heavily fortified, as was a tobacco factory near the middle, It was from these two strong-points that the stiffest opposition was expected to come.

With the Essex Scottish and the Hamilton Light Infantry, engineers were to land and dynamite parts of the concrete sea-wall so that Calgary tanks which were to follow the infantry would be able to get up the beach to the town. The Fusiliers Mont-Royal were to be held as a floating reserve, and an hour after the two infantry battalions and the tanks were ashore this regiment was to be sent in.

While the landings were taking place fighter planes and bombers of the RAF, US Army Air Forces and other Allied air forces in Britain were to come into action. The fighters were to go inland to intercept enemy fighter aircraft and bombers before they could come out to the coast to attack the men on the beaches and the ships and landing craft off-shore.

Our bombers were to bomb aerodromes behind Dieppe and attack troop concentrations, railway and road junctions, and highways to hinder reinforcements being brought up. Army Co-operation planes were to assist them in reconnaissance.

The land forces were under the command of Major-General J. H. Roberts, chief of the Canadian Second Division. The naval force commander was Captain J. Hughes-Hallet, R.N., and the air force commander was Air Marshal T. Leigh-Mallory. General Roberts and Captain Hughes-Hallet were to have their headquarters in the leading craft of the flotilla, the destroyer H.M.S. *Calpe*, and Air Marshal Leigh-Mallory was to conduct air activities from Fighter Command Headquarters in Britain. Once the operation got under way there was to be constant two-way wireless communication between the men on shore, the headquarters ship and other vessels off-shore, and headquarters staff in England.

It did not enter into the plan that if all went well Dieppe would be used as a bridgehead for a greater landing force. The Germans gave out after the raid that it had been the first step in a full-scale invasion that had fizzled out. This was not the case. It was a raid purely and simply, and the transport ships and other craft were to lie off-shore while the fighting as going on and then come in later in the day to disembark the land forces.

III

Planning the raid and specially training the forces engaged had gone on for months before it took place.

In the actual planning of the operation there were six main factors to bear in mind: first, the weather, tide, moon, and so on; second, how long it would take the Germans to get their reinforcements up into the area; third, air cover; fourth, sea patrols; fifth the composition of the attacking forces; sixth, security.

As far as the weather and the tides were concerned, it seems hardly necessary to point out that a raid such as this can't be attempted any old time. For the troops to be successfully landed it was essential to have ideal weather conditions, as high a tide as possible, and a dark night preceding the day of the raid, so that transports could be moved up with the least possibility of being observed. Had weather been bad, rain would have spoiled the visibility for the land forces and the planes overhead, and heavy winds would have made the seas rough and landings hazardous. The tide had to be high, because the beaches of Dieppe slope down quite sharply for fifty yards or so from the shore and then flatten out. When the tide is in the water is deep right in close to the shore. When it's out there's a broad stretch of shallow water in which landing craft would run aground and not be able to disembark and embark troops without the likelihood of getting stuck.

For the landing craft to function smoothly, then, it was necessary to have a high tide. But Dame Nature has worked things out so that full tides and full moons go hand in hand. Therefore, if the raid had been planned to take place on the morning of a full tide it would have meant approaching Dieppe in the light of a full moon.

However, there are certain times of the month when the moon, practically full, comes up and down early in the evening. Such a night was August 18, the night before the raid. The moon disappeared from the heavens at about one in the morning, ensuring darkness for the ships as they advanced towards the French coast. Also, the tide was due in about dawn, and though not exactly a full tide, it was high enough to provide plenty of freeboard for the landing craft when they put their nose aground.

All of that was quite a meteorological problem to get straightened out before any of the other planning of the raid was got into.

The important factor of how long it would take the Germans to bring up their reinforcements hinged on the accuracy of our air reconnaissance and intelligence services. The Nazi system of defence along these coasts had been worked out by Field Marshal von

Rundstedt, Commander-in-Chief of the German forces occupying western Europe. Von Rundstedt had been faced with the problem of having an extremely long coastline to defend and only some thirty divisions to do it with.

The system he worked out was to a have a series of very strong forts along the coast. These forts, and other pill-boxes and strong-points, were designed to blast troops as they attempt to land. There are not large bodies of troops deployed in this forward area. They are stationed inland at key points. From these centres the reinforcements can be rushed to the coast to engage the invaders at whatever point they land.

From air reconnaissance and intelligent reports those who planned the operation had to figure out as accurately as possible what strength of land forces there was in the Dieppe area and how long it would take the Germans to move up into Dieppe itself.

IV

In the consideration of providing adequate air cover for our ground fighting men, another important factor was present.

Not only did we want to protect the men and ships from attack from the air, but we also hoped to have a large-scale battle with the Luftwaffe. The enemy could ill afford to lose a large number of planes and pilots. So, when the news came through that the Allies had landed in Dieppe, the Luftwaffe seemed to have three alternatives, First of all, they could have ignored the operation from an aerial point of view and concentrated on trying to overcome the visitors with land troops only. Or secondly, they could have put into the air all the planes they had available at aerodromes in the vicinity and treated it as a local engagement. Or finally, they could have brought everything they could possibly spare from the whole of western Europe, to bring a really large force intro the locality.

It was the third alternative they chose, which was just what we wanted them to do. As a matter of fact, looking back on the thing now, it looks as though the German air chiefs went into a grand and glorious tail-spin. They panicked. They rushed planes from all over

Occupied France, from Belgium, Germany, even from Holland. They even used night-fighters and night-bombers. Anything and everything they put into commission.

In this way the Germans showed their hand, showed us much more clearly that we could ever have learned by other means just what state her air power in the west was in. It was necessary that we should know what first-line planes and reserves they could summon before we went into North Africa.

No only did we learn what superiority we had in numbers of aircraft, but also we inflicted in the air battle of Dieppe terrific damage on that limited German air strength. As I have mentioned in another part of this book, we were able to destroy definitely 170 enemy planes, with the loss to ourselves of 106 aircraft. If there were certain aspects of the Dieppe raid that were not entirely satisfactory from our point of view, the victory we won in the air on August 19 was an outstanding achievement.

An interesting point is that at Dieppe our planes set out to do much the same type of thing as did the Germans in the Battle of Britain. We launched vast numbers of fighters and bombers over enemy territory in daylight. The dog-fights that ensured were comparable to those in the skies over southern England in the latter part of the summer of 1940. But with his difference. The battle was not won by the defending force, as it had been in the Battle of Britain, but by the attacking force.

In the Battle of Britain we had the advantage of fighting over our own territory, while the enemy had to come a hundred miles or so, which placed them on such limitations as that on the time fighter aircraft could spend in the air before having to return to base to refuel. But at Dieppe we in turn were the invading air force, and any advantage accruing from fighting above your own aerodromes was enjoyed by the Germans. Yet we were able to lick them thoroughly again.

One can only say God knows what sort of shambles Dieppe would have been had we not been able to gain air supremacy. Granted some enemy planes did get through to bomb and machine-gun us, but it was nothing compared to the lambasting that would have been our lot had the enemy superiority in the air.

Chapter 3

A Convoy Disrupts the Plan

I

I have outlined the plan of attack. Now what actually hapened?

The ships set out on schedule from the south coast of England on the Tuesday night. They got well across the Channel without incident. But a little after three o'clock in the morning the ships on the left flank of our advancing flotilla encountered a German convoy coming down the Channel. A battle ensured. This did not affect the ships in the centre or on the right flank; those ships went on through the darkness.

The sea battle didn't last long – only about twenty minutes. But it had a profound effect on the whole operation. It threw the raid out of plumb. It meant that the ships carrying the troops which were to land on the left flank – at Berneval and Puys – were held up for twenty minutes. They were unable to make up for lost time and arrive on schedule at 4.50, as the No. 4 Commando and the South Saskatchewan Regiment (with whom I went in) did at Varengeville and Pourville.

The Germany convoy, which suffered heavily in the short engagement, turned tail and headed back up-Channel. They had no idea what they had run into, had no inkling that it was one flank of a vast array of transport ships, invasion barges, and escort craft headed for a raid on the French coast.

After the raid it was held by many people that the Germans had known that we were coming, that they had foreknowledge of the whole thing, and that they were waiting for us to show our noses.

This is definitely not so. Granted they were ready for us in that they expected something might happen for some time along the coast, but just where and precisely when they did not know, as was proved by various things.

After the convoy encounter out at sea our troops assailing the left flank arrived late. In broad daylight instead of just when dawn was breaking. By the time they arrived we on the right flank had already been ashore for about half an hour. By then the Germans knew something was on, and were at their guns ready when No. 3 Commando and the Royal Regiment of Canada arrived. Had these units on the left flank not been held up they would have taken the enemy by surprise as we were able to do at Varengeville and Pourville. Not a single shot was fired at us as we went up the beach, and a goodly proportion of the Nazi troops we had to rouse out of their beds with bayonets. Had the enemy known all about it, as some people maintain, they surely would have been at their posts ready for us.

Not only did the Germans not know beforehand that we were coming, but it seemed clear that the German convoy out at sea, thinking the ships they had run into were merely a Channel convoy, had not notified the coastal batteries that invasion barges were on their way towards the coast of France.

Other critics have asked why the operation wasn't called off when we met the enemy convoy. Well, for one thing, we were only a few miles off the coast at the time. How could the men on hundreds of ships have been told to turn about and head home? Wireless silence was being observed until we landed. To give out the order by wireless would have given our position away to the enemy, and they would have immediately set their shore batteries and aircraft on us. Nor would it have been practical to notify the ships in the flotilla by signal lamps. This would have given us away.

Had the raid been called off then it also would have provided the Axis with a grand and glorious opportunity to deride the Allies. The news of the raid that didn't come off would surely have leaked out in some way, and the United Nations would have been the laughing-stock of the world.

I mentioned above, as one of the important factors in the planning of the raid, the matter of security. The secret of Dieppe was well kept, despite the numbers of troops engaged and the long months of training that these troops underwent before they embarked.

The Canadians did their training on a strip of coastline that approximates very closely to that of the Dieppe area. They moved in there with units of the Royal Navy whose job it was going to be to take them to Dieppe and get them back again. They rehearsed all the landings over and over again, separately and all together, carrying out in theory the whole raid, from start to finish.

Just how thoroughly the troops were schooled before they tackled the job was brought home to me on the streets of Pourville. I wanted to get to a certain part of the town. I asked an officer if he knew how I could reach the British Hotel. He told me at once, 'You go fifty yards along this street, turn to the left, and it's just across the square.' He had never been to Pourville in his life. But a model of Dieppe and its surrounding townships had been built for the officers to study during their training for the raid. It was built exactly to scale. Every street, square, and building was there. They studied that model so thoroughly that by the time they arrived on the scene the place was almost as familiar to them as their own home-town.

II

The fact the units on the left flank arrived late, to be greeted by a barrage of fire from the shore, meant that the No. 3 Commando was unable to land and put the six heavy artillery guns at Berneval out of action. On the right flank all went well. The No. 4 Commando landed, captured the garrison, spiked the guns, and blew up the ammunition stores. That made sure we weren't molested from that quarter. At Berneval, however, the guns never were silenced, and the German gun-crews were able to keep up quite a steady fire on the men on the beaches and on the ships off-shore.

Some men of the No. 3 Commando were able to get ashore, and they took up positions in the cornfields from which they could snipe at the German gunners. This harassed them, and though not having the desired effect of wiping those six guns out of the operation, it at least cut down their efficiency.

The Royal Regiment of Canada, rebuffed at their first attempt to land at Puys, formed up again, and made other assaults on the headland. But the strong-points above Dieppe on the eastern cliff were not overcome, and their barrage of fire, combined with that of the artillery guns about five miles farther east at Berneval, accounted for much of the hell that descended on the main beach at Dieppe and at Pourville, about a mile and a half along to the west. This was the result of that stroke of bad luck – tangling with the German convoy out on the Channel. Had it not happened Dieppe would have been a very different story.

It just shows how much hinges on the element of surprise. If your surprise attack comes off – well and good. But some small, unforeseen incident can happen, and the whole operation will be threatened.

The entire Dieppe raid was built on the premise that we should take the enemy by surprise. That is the main reason why we didn't bomb the defences heavily before our troops landed.

Some critics have asked why heavy bombers weren't sent in to pound Dieppe before the land forces were put ashore. One reason is that we wanted to avoid as much as possible endangering the lives of the French people. But, as I shall mention later on, the main tactical reason was that if we had raided the town before attacking we should have awakened every German soldier in the vicinity. They all would have been up and about, on the alert, and any chance of getting ashore unbeknown to them would have disappeared. Also, the enemy would have been warned that something was afoot, and reinforcements in the rear would have been rushed up to prepare for eventualities. We should have arrived to find a substantial welcoming party awaiting us.

Nevertheless there is no doubt about the fact bombers dropping some really heavy bombs, perhaps some of the 8,000-pounders, would have been much more effective against the Germans forts than any form of action we did take against them.

These concrete forts, with walls several feet thick, are able to withstand a terrific amount of punishment. It would seem that about the only thing that would demolish them is accurate bombing with large bombs or heavy artillery fire. The way we tried to immobilize them at Dieppe was by ground troops capturing them, using Commando stealth methods of overcoming gun-crews. This was not entirely successful.

We went to Dieppe to test the enemy defences, and that was one of the lessons we learned.

III

No paratroops were landed at any stage of the operations. Dieppe was attacked first upon the flanks and then by a frontal assault. No attempts were made to tackle the town from behind. If paratroops had been dropped behind the town, it was doubtful whether they would have been of very much use. They would have landed in the thick of the enemy's rearward troop concentrations. They would have had little chance of survival, let alone getting anything done.

The Germans had strengthened their forces all along the coast. Our Intelligence Services had found that out. New units had been moved up just a few days before the raid took place. That fact was also put forward as an indication that the Germans knew we were coming. But it was not only in the Dieppe area that the defences had been strengthened by additional troops. It was the case all along the coast. With things not going well for the Russians on the Soviet front, the Germans were expecting action of some sort from us in the west, and had made special precautions.

After the No. 4 Commando and the South Saskatchewan and Winnipeg Cameron Regiments had landed successfully on the right flank, and the No. 3 Commando and the Royal Regiment had done their best to get ashore on the left, the infantry and tanks landed on the main beach as scheduled. As the landing craft bringing troops and tanks advanced to the beach they were met with withering fire from the cliffs, and the tobacco factory and the casino on the shoreline.

Landing craft were sunk, many of the men were killed by machine-gun fire before they even touched the beach, but nevertheless the assault was carried through. After bitter fighting the casino was taken, and other strong-points along the front of the beach were silenced.

The engineers, working under a hail of fire, were able to blow up part of the sea-wall, in preparation for the tanks. The first wave of tanks was landed on the beach, and their heavy guns went into action. Soon some of them were able to get up in to the Esplanade and across into the town.

In their reports of the raids the Germans claimed that none of our tanks had been able to get off the beach. Not only was that a definite lie, but the Germans themselves proved, in a poorly done piece of propaganda, that our tanks had penetrated quite a distance inland. This was in some of the leaflets they dropped in Britain about a week after the raid. The leaflets were dropped in their thousands in the South of England, where the Canadians are stationed.

The leaflet was a four-page document about magazine size. It contained twenty-eight photographs taken on the beaches and around the town after the raid. Most of the photographs were of our tanks, and prisoners the Germans had taken. One of the photographs showed a tank in a tank-trap. It was probably meant to demonstrate how effective the Germans' precautions against tanks had been, but the interesting point about the picture was the fact that there was no sign whatsoever of the beach in it. There were buildings and grassland around the tank-trap, and in the distance were wooded hills and farms. The tank had obviously penetrated well up the shore.

Incidentally, another interesting point about this leaflet was that by showing photographs of hundreds of Canadian prisoners the Germans hoped to demoralize their companions back in England. But this was another case of Nazi propaganda back-firing. The Canadian troops who had got back safe and sound from the raid were worried about the fate of many of their pals. But in these photographs they could identify many of them, and saw them to be none the worse for the events of the battle, except that they were prisoners. Rather than demoralizing our men in England, the Germans had done them a good turn quite unintentionally.

At Dieppe we hoped to have a real test of our ability to land tanks, and we wanted to see whether or not out tank-landing craft as designed were the right type of vessel for the job. Though we did run into many difficulties getting our tanks ashore, the tank-landing craft proved themselves, and the very fact of our running into snags answered for us the questions that can only be answered by putting things to the test of actual battle.

We paid a heavy price in men and material. Over two thousand men failed to come back from the raid. What proportion of those who were killed is not known definitely as yet. Nor is the number of Germans that were killed known. The casualties were by no means only on the Allied side. When the figures do come out, which probably won't be until after the War, it will no doubt be seen that the casualties we suffered were by no means out of proportion to those of the enemy, remembering that we were the attacking force.

IV

In the pages that follow I relate the story of the raid as I experienced it, from the time we left England to our return.

On the raid I was a guest in every sense of the word. A non-combatant, I was not permitted to take an active part in the action. I had undergone no previous training with the troops before they embarked. I was a civilian invited along to observe the proceedings. The following chapters are a personal record of my impressions and reactions, and I have tried to give a frank account of how it feels to step out of everyday life and go with an invading force undertaking a raid.

I had come to England early in 1941 and had been covering the activities of the Canadian Army stationed in Britain for my paper, the *Montreal Standard*. After eighteen months I was beginning to share the feelings of the troops themselves. 'When are we going to see some action?'

Then on Tuesday afternoon, August 18, we found ourselves at the dock gates of a South of England port...

Chapter 4

We Leave for France

I

At the dock gates they told me which of the troop-ships I was going on, and at five o'clock I went aboard. The ship was heavily camouflaged with tarpaulins so that nobody on the wharves could see what was going on board, and she remained camouflaged like this throughout our passage down the estuary out to sea. I know that definitely, because I wanted to take a last look back at the coast of England as we steamed away, and I remember the trouble I had finding a gap in those tarpaulins through which I could get a good view.

Most of the troops were aboard when I arrived, and they were being issued with iron rations, being 'briefed' by their commanding officers and platoon commanders, cleaning their rifles, and doing a hundred and other preparatory jobs. It was a hot, sunny afternoon, but under the tarpaulins it was cool and shady, and as I walked along the deck to report to the captain my eye caught the glint of metal in the shadows. It was a group of soldiers sharpening their bayonets.

As I paused a moment a burly-looking farmer from Saskatchewan held out his bayonet and said, 'Just feel the edge on that. I've waited a long time to cut me a slice of Hun. I guess I'm just the bloodthirsty type.'

The regiment I was attached to was the South Saskatchewan Regiment, infantrymen mostly made up of farmers. Their Intelligence Officer took me in hand and gave me an envelope marked 'Secret'. On opening it I found it contained three maps of Dieppe and district.

This was the first intimation I got it was Dieppe we were going to raid. When Major Cliff Wallace, Public Relations Officer for the Canadian Army, had got us war correspondents together and outlined the raid to us, he had referred to it merely as a town on the French coast.

II

The first news I got that I was going on a raid was a telephone call I had from Major Wallace in London on the Friday. He called me up from his hotel and said, 'Can you come down here at once? I want to talk to you confidentially.'

As I seated myself in his hotel bedroom he poked his head out of the door and took a look up and down the hall. He tapped the walls of the room and looked out of the window to make sure there was no chance of our voices carrying across the light wall. With a smile he turned to me and remarked, 'This all seems very melodramatic and "secret service" but this is the real thing this time, and you can't be too careful.'

Seating himself on the edge of the bed, Major Wallace said quietly, 'Do you feel pretty fit?'

I told him that by Army standards I didn't suppose I was particularly fit.

'But by war correspondents' standards you're okay, eh? Well, would you like to go on a trip? It's going to be pretty strenuous, and it's going to be dangerous. But it's going to be the biggest Canadian Army story that's broken so far in this war, and we should like to have you along.'

I said, 'Okay, fine,' and he told us be at a certain railway station the following afternoon at 3.30. Besides my regular army uniform I was going to need a water-bottle, a compass, and numerous other extras. I said I should be able to buy these easily enough next morning, and here I was to get an insight into the stringent security precautions that have to be taken on an operation such as this. Major Wallace told me that on no account was I to buy this equipment in a West End store.

'We mustn't give anybody the opportunity of putting two and two together,' he said. 'Besides the service chiefs and the war correspondents there are only three or four other people in the country who know this thing is on. If one of your friends were to see you buying a water-bottle, he might say to himself, "Why is Reyburn buying a water-bottle? There must be something on."'

Even when we correspondents got to the railway station next day we were given no inkling of the type of operation we were going on. The Conducting Officer merely handed us tickets to a town in the South of England.

III

Twenty correspondents and official photographers accompanied the troops to Dieppe, and this was the largest group of pressmen ever to go on such an undertaking. For the few days before we boarded our ships we were split up into groups of five or six and sent to various parts of England handy to the South Coast ports from which we were going to leave. There were five others besides myself in the party I was with. Over a few beers in our hotel each evening we would get several major issues of the war straightened out to our satisfaction, but failed to guess correctly the exact nature of the story we were about to cover. There was Drew Middleton, a lively, youthful, rotund New Yorker who was covering the raid for Associated Press and has since joined the staff of *The New York Times*. Fred Griffin, oldest of us all, is an Irish Canadian who'd been writing articles for his paper, *Toronto Daily Star*, when we were still in our cradles. Ross Munro was the Canadian Press man on the show. He'd been living with the Canadian Army and writing news articles and feature articles about them since the day they arrived in England. Twenty-eight years of age, tall, bespectacled and earnest, Munro had earned through his dispatches a high regard from the Canadian authorities, and it was to turn out that his stories were among the best writing to come out of Dieppe. Lieutenant Frank Royle, former *Winnipeg Free Press* photographer, was the official Canadian Army cameraman. His pictures got the best play of any taken on the raid. Canadian radio was represented by Bob Bowman, well known in England as well as Canada before the war as an ice-hockey commentator.

War correspondents, though they wear regular uniforms and are under the discipline of the Army in the field, are not actually in the Army. They have the privileges but not the rank of a captain and wear no insignia except their war correspondent shoulder tabs. They are non-combatants and do not carry arms of any sort.

While we were in this English town for four days waiting for this raid to start it was suspected local people might suspect that something was in the wind if they saw a cluster of war correspondents strolling round the place. So before we left London we were told to take our war correspondent's tabs off and put some pips up for the time being. Ross Munro emerged as a major, most of the others were first lieutenants, but Fred Griffin came into our midst as a 'one pipper'. About fifty years of age and getting rather thin on top, Griffin became the centre of a lot of good-humoured banter, particularly when he walked through the town beside the youthful 'Major' Munro. His comment on the situation was, 'When these people see an old buffer like me walking around with just one pip they must say to themselves, "Golly, where's that guy been all his life?"' On the second day we 'promoted' Fred Griffin to major.

It wasn't until the day before the raid – on the Tuesday – that we learned when it was going to come off or were given any idea of just what was going to happen. Major Wallace joined us and around noon took us to a lonely orchard on the edge of town. We seated ourselves in an old summer-house, and a sentry was posted outside pretending to be looking over the apple crop but keeping a watchful eye there were no eavesdroppers.

Major Wallace drew a rough map of the beaches of Dieppe but didn't name it. We were told what the objectives of the raid were, how a large force was going to be landed, and which regiments we were going with. Previously to this we had no real feeling of tension and excitement. We just knew we were going to be on a big story, and it was a matter of waiting until the 'balloon went up'. But now we could feel a mounting surge of expectancy, a thrill at the audacity and brilliant planning of the raid, a feeling that we were going on something really big.

IV

So as I opened up those maps on the ship I learned for the first time we were bound for Dieppe.

As we sat down to supper the ship slipped out from the wharf, and we headed out into the Channel. I was seated beside the Colonel of the Regiment, Lieutenant-Colonel C.C.I. Merritt. This was the first time I'd ever met Colonel Merritt, but on the following day I was to see him display inspired leadership and perform acts of bravery that undoubtedly placed him among the great war heroes of Canada. He became Canada's first V.C. of the war.

Ces Merritt was only thirty-three years of age. It is the expressed policy of the Canadian Army to have young commanding officers in the field, and testimony to this is the fact that the average age of lieutenant-colonels was thirty-two. Before Dieppe there were sarcastic remarks about the youthfulness of many of the colonels in the Canadian Army. In fact, in one mess a notice was pinned over the bar which read, 'Drinks will not be served to Canadian colonels under twenty-one, unless accompanied by their parents.'

That this young-officer policy was sound was proved at Dieppe. The way Colonel Merritt conducted himself in action was typical of how all the young officers served in the operation.

Merritt is tall, very powerfully built – he looks like a solid Rugby forward – with short hair, a moustache, and strong, clear-cut features. He was extremely popular with his men, who all spoke of him as 'a helluva fine fellow.' He was friendly, easy to get to know, a good mixer. A boyish grin and a certain self-consciousness on occasions were the only keys to his youthfulness.

He hails from Vancouver, British Columbia, and started his career there as a lawyer. In 1935 he gave up law for the Army and studied at the famed Royal Military College, in Kingston, Ontario. His wife and children are living in Ontario now, and from Mrs Grace Merritt I received a cable a few days after Dieppe. She had read my account of what he did in the *Montreal Standard* and asked for any news I could give her of him. I wrote her a long letter and later was able to visit her in Canada and tell her the whole story in person.

The best way to describe how his fellow-officers felt about Merritt is for me to repeat what I heard one officer say to another at the supper-table. He said, 'You've got to put a drag-rope on the Colonel to keep up with him.'

Over a cup of coffee Colonel Merritt explained to me what his regiment's job was going to be at Dieppe. The South Saskatchewans were to go in at dawn – at ten minutes to five. We were to land at Pourville Beach, which is a mile or so to the west of Dieppe proper and is a continuation of the main beach. We were to be the first troops to land, and our task was to form a perimeter, then to solidify each flank on either side of the valley formed by the river, and thus form a passage-way for the Winnipeg Regiment of the Camerons of Canada. They were to land half an hour after us.

Though he had a thousand and one things to think about at this time, it was typical of Merritt to take time out to put straight for me a little problem I had in mind. I asked him for his advice as to whether, as a war correspondent. I should carry a weapon or not.

I had 'Canada War Correspondent' on the flap of my tunic, but I had visualized the possibility of coming face to face with a Nazi, rifle in hand, and I'd point to the insignia and explain as quickly as possible that I was merely as an observer, not as a combatant. It struck me that in a case like that the trigger-finger would always be quicker than the tongue.

But Merritt said, 'I'd advise you definitely not to be armed. There's an international agreement on this thing, and if you're captured and any weapons are found on you you'll be treated as a man using his non-combatant status to take advantage of the enemy. You'd be put up against a wall and shot – just like that.'

I thanked the Colonel and departed, trying to figure out in my mind what this all added up to. If I didn't carry arms I was as likely to be slugged as anybody else; if I did carry arms and was captured I'd be shot anyway. Whatever way you looked at it there didn't seem much future in it.

Nevertheless I took Colonel Merritt's advice.

V

After supper those of us who didn't already have them were issued with life-belts. They were of the naval type which I'd encountered before, when I did a convoy trip on a destroyer on the North Atlantic patrol. The naval life-belt consisted of a rubber tube about five inches wide and long enough to go once around the chest. Covered with white canvas, it has a neck-band to keep it well under the armpits and a long rubber nozzle for blowing it up.

A naval officer on the ship who'd been in the Navy all his life and had been thankful for his life-belt on more than one occasion during the war gave me some tips how to wear it. Keep it blown up all the time, he told me, and don't wait until you get into the water to do the blowing up. Have it as high on your chest as possible, he added, or you'll have your bottom floating on the surface and your head under water.

All the troops wore their life-belts throughout the engagement, while landing, while fighting in the streets, and coming out. I can see now that this naval officer's advice to me about keeping my life-belt blown up all the time probably saved my life. When we were leaving the beaches and had to jump from one sinking landing craft into the water to swim to another I didn't realize at the time that my heavy army equipment would have probably sent me to the bottom. In the rush and bustle of getting off that beach it wouldn't have occurred to me to take time out to blow up my life-belt. But having already been inflated, it kept me up in the water.

As well as the life-belts we were all issued with a bag of sandwiches to eat ashore. I never got round to eating mine. All I ate the ten hours we were in Dieppe – from the time we landed until we left the scene in a destroyer – was half a two-ounce Nestlé's chocolate bar. Most of us gave any chocolate we had to the French people we met when we arrived, chocolate being something they hadn't seen for months.

The reason I didn't eat the sandwiches was because they became what might be termed contaminated during action. What happened was this. When the barrage of enemy mortar and artillery fire was at its highest I was at a temporary clearing-station for the wounded. It was a grass plot by a concrete building. To get the best possible shelter we lay close to the wall. As mortar shells burst out on the street just in front of us our heads went down and into the grass so that out tins hats would give us the maximum protection.

I noticed that the grass was damp and smelled rather. My sandwiches were trucked in my jacket and I soon realized that they wouldn't be fit to eat. It wasn't rain that had made the grass wet – some of our troops had chosen that particular spot to relieve themselves.

A sidelight on this incident is the evidence it provides that a habit such as the choice of location for such proceedings dies hard, even with soldiers in the height of battle.

VI

I went down below-decks after supper to grab a bit of sleep. The 'tween-decks of the transport ship were crowded with troops. The air was close and laden with tobacco smoke, because all the port-holes were blacked out, and there was little ventilation. Some of the men were lying huddled on the steel floor, sleeping. Others were fusing grenades, loading Bren-gun and Sten-gun magazine, oiling their rifles thoroughly to guard against the salt water jamming the works. Some of the men were clustered round platoon commanders, getting final briefing instructions.

The lads were in fine shape, just rarin' to go. I remember wondering as I walked round among them what the Germans are like when they go into battle. Taken by and large, the German soldier is a stolid, humourless individual. These Canadian soldiers, though they obviously weren't treating the matter in hand as a joke, managed to introduce lots of laughter, leg-pulling, and banter into their preparations for battle.

Maybe they joked merely to relive the tension inside them. But I think it's just something inherent in their make-up, this ability to retain their sense of humour. Whether you go among English and Dominion pilots at fighter and bomber stations, into the deserts of the Middle East among the New Zealand and Australian troops, among the Navy and merchant seamen on the convoys, whether you talk to your London Cockney after a Blitz, it's there all the time. I recall the story of a Cockney woman after the May 10 London raid. She was sweeping away the glass from the pavement in front of her battered shop. As she swept she muttered to herself, 'I'm sick and tired of being Hitler's bloody housemaid, clearing up after him like this.'

As I passed down to the lower deck, where there was a cabin I was going to sleep in, I heard one of the lads say something that was typical of their conversation at this time. He was talking about a friend of his who hadn't come on the raid. 'If I get bumped off,' he said. 'Bert is going to be mad as hell, because I owe him a shilling.'

I snatched only an hour or so's sleep in the cabin. It was right alongside the engine-room. Like most of the other men in the ship, I was keyed up at the prospect of going into action for the first time in my life. But as if that wasn't enough, as I lay on the bunk smoking a cigarette before I dozed off, I watched the smoke I expelled from my lungs and the ship was vibrating so much that that smoke didn't just hang in the air as most well-behaved cigarette smoke does. It vibrated back and forth. An eerie effect, smoke shaking in the atmosphere.

I was awakened by a steward who told me that everybody on the lower deck had to come up on top – we were passing through an enemy mine field.

VII

It was around midnight now, and I went up on to the top deck. It was a glorious night, cool and clear, the sky laden with stars, an almost full moon on the starboard side casting a broad ribbon of golden light on the water. The motor-landing craft and the assault landing craft were slung from davits on the deck, and I climbed up on to the flat top of an A.L.C.

There was a soldier sitting there by himself, and I sat down beside him. I couldn't make out his features, and if I saw Reg (as I found out his name was) to-morrow I shouldn't be able to recognize him.

You just naturally reach for a cigarette at a time like this, but I checked myself when I remembered the no-smoking on deck order.

Reg looked out across the swath of moonlit water and said, 'Look at that moon. A cool summer evening and your ship slipping through the water and the moonlight following you along as you go. On a pleasure ship on the lakes back home this'd be romantic stuff, wouldn't it? Same setting exactly, but this is kinda different, isn't it?'

He told me about Bernice, and how he was going to marry her if he got back in one piece. She was a school-teacher near Maryfield, in Saskatchewan, where he had worked on his family's farm. She hadn't fancied his coming overseas, but he joined up a couple of days after war was declared without telling her. He'd just gone off to the recruiting office and turned up in uniform one day as Bernice was locking up the country school.

He was a sound, leavel-headed sort of chap, Reg. He must have been only about twenty. He hadn't joined up just for the chance of adventure. He knew even out there in the security of the lonely prairies what was at stake over in Europe, and he was willing to offer his life.

I have no way of knowing what happened to Reg at Dieppe, but if by any chance he didn't come back I want to go and find that school near Maryfield and tell Bernice what was in Reg's thoughts when he went into action. Two and a half years is a long time when you're young. There must have been dozens of times when she thought to herself, 'Reg is over there in England, and he's probably getting lonesome ... and there are lots of English girls ... He'll no doubt forget all about me.'

When we were landing on the beaches I caught a glimpse of a locket one of the boys was wearing pinned to his tunic. It wasn't a locket really. It was an empty watch-face with a snapshot of a girl placed inside. Bernice and Mary and Helen and Joyce and all the others back home ... they weren't forgotten.

Chapter 5

We Go Ashore

I

After a final meal the order came in the morning for us to embark in the landing craft.

The troops formed up below-decks in their platoons and sections. Their faces under their netted tin hats were wet with perspiration from the close atmosphere in the ship and the weight of the equipment they were bearing. Naturally burly and of fine physique, these farmers and ranchers from Saskatchewan were made to look even more formidable by their full equipment. The life-belts under their tunics built out their chests to huge proportions; from the shoulders of some of them hung the ropes which were to help us climb up the twelve-foot sea-wall from the beach on to the promenade; hand-grenades dangled from their belts; Bren guns, Sten guns and rifles were slung over their shoulders; long knives hung from their hips; revolver holsters were at the ready; mortar shells bulged in the webbing of the mortar crews; Tommy-guns were crooked under the forearms of the section leaders.

I took a good firm grip of my notebook and pencil, said to myself that here was the one time that the man who said 'the pen is mightier than the sword' was a liar, and we headed for the boats.

The moon had gone down, and it was quite dark on deck now. The men were going up ladders into the barges, and from where we were standing below, the figures of the soldiers already up there formed striking silhouettes against the star-studded sky.

I was going ashore with the second-in-command of the Regiment, Major J. E. McRae, a former customs official from Weyburn, Saskatchewan. Our barge was a motor-landing craft which differs in many ways from an assault landing craft. Designed to accommodate

Bren-gun carriers and army vehicles as well as personnel, the M.L.C. is about fifty feet long and fifteen feet wide. The hull is steel, the sides are about waist high. The front ramp, which is lowered when the craft touches the beach, is about eighty foot high; the engines are in the stern. The main difference in an A.L.C., which is used only for landing personnel, is that the sides are higher and there is a covering of steel which affords protection to those inside.

As we were lowered overboard from the davits there was a call from the ship, 'You're on your own now – give 'em hell!'

Our 'mother ship' steamed away, and we were in our barges in the Channel there, headed for the French coast. We had a fair journey ahead of us.

Though it was difficult to see very clearly in the darkness, we could make out the shapes of dozens of other barges skimming along with us, and special craft, signalling to us, shepherding us together very much like a duck watching over her ducklings. It was the Navy at work. It was their job to get us in there on time and at the right landing-places. I'll have more to say later about the magnificent part the British Navy played at Dieppe. Sufficient now to record the precision and thoroughness with which they carried out their task. Quite frankly, when it comes to writing about the British Navy in action, what words one can summon to mind – words like 'magnificent', 'terrific', 'outstanding', 'inspiring' – seem hopelessly inadequate One longs for a new batch of brand-new descriptive words of praise that nobody has ever used before and which give a true idea how one feels about the Navy.

The bow of our craft was throwing up a fine spray, and it felt cool and refreshing on our faces. The men undid their gas capes and spread them over themselves to keep the salt water away from their weapons and equipment.

Suddenly – so suddenly and unexpectedly that it gave us a start – the whole sky was lighted up from behind us, over to the north-east. It was a flare. We watched it ride slowly down to the water's edge, and it seemed to light up the whole Channel … and us with it.

Then we were treated to the sight of as tracer-bullet battle that, regarded from the purely visual point of view, was more colourful than any of us had seen at a July the Fourth fireworks display. At that time we didn't know very clearly what it was all about, but even though we sensed that some of our boys were in trouble we couldn't help but be fascinated by the sight of the criss-crossing bursts of golden balls of fire, interspersed every now and then by rocket-shell explosions that burst into vivid red sprays of light.

It wasn't until we got home that we learned that a Germany convoy had had a chance encounter with the ships on our left flank.

We watched the whole battle going on for twenty minutes, quite at a loss to know what it was all about. Then all darkness again, and there was no further incident until we reached the beach.

The first streaks of dawn were starting to appear as we came nearer to the shore. We could pick out the cliffs now, and the men came to the alert, taking up crouching positions on the steel bottom of the barge and cocking their weapons.

Someone made us all laugh by remarking, 'If there a couple of lovers having a bit of fun there on the beach they're going to get one helluva surprise!'

His neighbour added, 'They'll say to themselves, 'Golly, we didn't know this was illegal.''

Most of us were down like sprinters ready for the hundred yards dash. I rested on one knee until it got sore and then transferred to the other. I adjusted my tin hat with superfluous frequency.

We could hear the water lapping on the beach now and could discern the shape of houses and hotels on the foreshore. The blackout was bad in one of the houses, and a light shone forth from a window. The man beside me ejaculated in a hushed whisper, 'Put that light out!'

There was the crunch of our craft touching on the beach, the ramp came down, and we dashed up the fifty yards of pebbles to the sea-wall.

Our heavy army boots on the pebbles made a lot of noise, and we felt that surely we must have awakened the whole town. But as we lay hard up against the parapet there was no sign that the enemy knew we were there. It was quite light now, and I could see the thin, long line of soldiers stretched along the whole length of the beach under the shelter of the twelve-foot wall. There was the dark, heavy smell of seaweed and salt water.

A thick mesh of barbed wire hung down from the top of the parapet to the pebbles.

II

At last the enemy had spotted us. The splatter of machine-guns broke out, and we edged closer to the wall. But no bullets seemed to land close to us. The Pourville Beach is long and straight, and the machine-gunners couldn't get the angle necessary to get at us where we were.

I found myself reclining on a strand of barbed wire and for some reason went to the trouble of examining it closely. It seemed different from any I had seen before. It appeared to be rustless, was very thick, and the barbs were big and ugly-looking. The wire-cutters were practically up to the top of the parapet now. They were clearly exposed to view from the town, and I felt sure would be picked off by snipers. I remember thinking at the time what guts a job like that takes.

The wire-cutters were having a hard time getting through. The wire was very well laid. It wasn't in uniform coils, but jammed together in a mess. They would cut strand after strand only to find it didn't make much difference like pulling at the threads of a hopelessly ravelled ball of string.

We seemed to be lying there for ages ... and we felt certain that at any moment we'd hear the clatter of boots up on the promenade, and the Germans would come to the edge of the parapet, stick their weapons over the top, and spray us with bullets.

Still the wire-cutters weren't through, and suddenly a call came from further down the line that they'd found an easy way to get up. We filed along and came to a place where there wasn't any barbed wire at all.

I gave the man in front of me a leg up and then clambered up myself, into a large blockhouse. When I got in there were thirty or forty of us there. It had thick concrete walls and was heavily sandbagged. It was quite empty and looked as if it had been for some time.

The thought suddenly flashed through my mind that it might be a trap. It had been too easy getting up that wall. The blockhouse was probably mined, and we'd all be blown to bits. I was to learn later that that blockhouse was mined, and it was a trap. Some of the Cameron Highlanders, who came in half an hour after us, climbed the wall the same way. When there was a bunch of them in the blockhouse somebody somewhere pressed a button, and the whole thing went up with them in it.

Why they didn't blow us up I don't know, but through the doorway now we could see our men advancing across the promenade. They signalled us that the coast was clear, and with Battalion Headquarters, I crossed the wide stretch of concrete and we established ourselves in an empty house.

All the houses and hotels along the promenade were empty, and, judging by the layers of dust and old, yellowed newspapers that lay about, they had been evacuated for some time. Behind our house was a large square of grass, fringed by low trees. It seemed to be a public park.

Our wireless set was put into action in the garage of the house, the operators sitting on the running boards of two large black cars, both of which were out of petrol and showed every sign of being laid up for the duration. We stood at the wide doorway and watched the platoons that were going to work house-clearing.

III

In the year and a half I'd been in England before Dieppe, writing articles for my paper on the training of the Canadian Army, I'd seen the infantrymen doing house-to-house-clearing practice dozens and dozens of times. In the fall of 1941, following the lead of some go-ahead young officers in a London Division, the Canadian Army had adopted the modern 'battle-drill' training. The idea behind the battle-drill was that too much time was wasted by the infantry doing parade-square drill (slope arms, form threes, right incline, etc.), and that time could be much better employed in teaching the men modern fighting methods.

What we call parade-square drill was in fact battle-drill but of another era. It's a hold-over from the days of the Napoleonic wars. In those times the weapons used by the infantry were far from accurate. The only way to get an anything like effective volley of fire was to line the men up in perfectly straight columns, dressed by the right. They were trained to load, aim, and fire by numbers. In that way they all fired at exactly the same moment, and through individually each soldier may not have been able to command much accuracy, the collective volley of fie sprayed forth a withering barrage – like machine-gun fire in waltz time.

Ever since those days the British armies have perpetuated the old battle orders in the form of parade-square routines. Though serving its purpose of 'making a soldier out of you,' it wasn't making you a *fighting* soldier in modern terms. So the Canadian Army, along with the Imperial and other Dominion Forces, have to all intents and purposes scrapped parade-square drill. In its place is battle-drill. No longer do the infantry 'number by the right'. Instead each man in a section has his allotted job; maybe he's the Tommy-gunner, Bren-gunner, a rifleman. Every tactic that could conceivably be employed in actual fighting has been given a signal word, and whether it's a matter of tackling an enemy strong-point or ousting the opposition from a wood or house-clearing, when this signal is passed on down every man knows automatically what his platoon or section is going to do and what his specific job in that operation will be. Just as he was drilled to proficiency in the old 'slope arms' formula, the modern infantryman is being taught by 'numbers' all the aspects of today's infantry fighting.

A good analogy is American rugby. It is just like a series of football plays. The platoon commander goes into a huddle with his section leaders, and they decide on the 'play' they are going to use. Like a rugby team, the troops have practised over and over again the dozens of different plays, and all they need are the cue-words to set them into action. Also, in a football manoeuvre, if things don't go quite as planned it's up to the individual to use his initiative. The men are encouraged to think for themselves and act on their own savvy, so the tendency in the old days for the foot-slogger to feel that he was just a cog in a wheel propelled by orders from the higher-ups has gone for ever.

If anyone had any doubts about the battle-drill being perfect training for modern war those doubts were dispelled at Dieppe.

Across the square from where I was standing I watched Tommy-gun and Bren-gun men keeping a house covered for their companions to go in They went forward and battered the door down with their rifle-butts, kicked through the windows at the side, and climbed in. It was the same stuff I had seen them do times without number at deserted houses near their training camps in England. Now here they were doing it with a precision and thoroughness that looked as though they'd been clearing enemy houses since the war began.

IV

Now I was to see the first Nazi soldier I'd ever set eyes on. He was brought from one of the houses, having been dislodged from his hiding place with hand-grenades. He wasn't young and he was bespectacled and rotund. He had the look of a man who had been talked into something; he hadn't ever wanted any part of this thing.

One of the grenades had torn away the flesh of his right shoulder and forearm, and as he was led up to us his left hand was holding a limp hand that was hanging from his body by mere shreds of tissue. There was not much questioning of a man in that condition, so he was taken off to get medical attention.

I remember reflecting as he was led away that I had always been squeamish at the sight of blood. To see anything like someone gashing his finger with a carving-knife always caused me to shudder. But for some reason what I had just seen brought no reaction. I concluded that in the excitement of battle you see such things and they don't fully record themselves on your mind ... until after it's all over, and then they come back to you.

From a neighbouring street more Nazi soldiers entered the square, walking in double file with their arms upraised. They were being brought in at the point of the bayonet. I know nobody looks their best when he has just been taken prisoner, but as these men were lined up for interrogation I couldn't help compare them with the Canadian soldiers who stood beside them. The Nazis were sullen-looking, pasty-faced and of poor physique. Most of them were old or very young – in other words what's left when you have taken away the cream of your man-power.

The Canadians, all of them in their early twenties, virile and powerfully built, were in striking contrast. But I checked myself from generalizing and later from the many others we came face to face within Dieppe that the enemy's troops were all of such poor calibre. Nevertheless it afforded a first-hand insight into the drain on man-power the Nazis are now confronted with.

I noticed the bayonet of one of the Canadians was covered with blood, and later I was to learn the story behind that. As they were bringing in the prisoners, this private, a lumberman named Silver Stuart from Moose Jaw, happened to catch sight of two German soldiers in a doorway of as house. Both of them had a stick grenade in each hand, and there were rifles propped up against the doorway ready for use. In a flash Stuart detached himself from his group and made a headlong dash at the Germans. With his bayonet he slashed both of them to ribbons. Leaving the bodies there, he rejoined his comrades without saying a word and marched here to Battalion Headquarters as if nothing had happened.

The prisoners' hands were not tied behind their backs as the Germans claimed a few days after Dieppe, when they threatened to place their British prisoners in irons until the War Office cancelled the alleged order to bind any prisoners so they that they couldn't destroy their papers. Incidentally, the German announcement was in the same genre as the one they put out about our obviously thinking that we were going to be able to march to the gates of Paris in triumph, because we took Union Jacks ashore with us. We did land with Union Jacks, and I saw plenty of them, but they were for the very practical purpose of draping them on any enemy vehicles we captured for our own use.

Chapter 6

In the Streets of Pourville

I

As I stood in the doorway of the garage I had a chance to take in the scene and get an idea of what this place we'd chosen as a battle-ground was like.

Pourville is really a suburb of Dieppe, its beach being separated from the main Dieppe beach by the mouth of a small river called the Scie. It is typical in appearance to the hundreds of other small watering-places dotted along the entire northern seaboard of France and Belgium. Holiday hotels (including the inevitable Grand) and *pensions* line the broad concrete walk we had just come across, and the town stretches inland for three or four blocks. It lies in the valley of the Scie, and low hills rise up from each side.

Facing inland as I was, I could see on the hilly, terraced land on the right of the river thick woods, dotted with hotels and summer cottages that I was told had often been occupied in peace-time by British and American tourists, families who used to move down from Paris during the summer. On the left side of the river and between Pourville and Dieppe proper is a golf course. The whole place is a pleasant little spot, with red-brick, grey-stone and wooden buildings, with white picket fences in front of the gardens.

The garage we'd set up headquarters in was a two-car affair, and its quota of cars was there all right. I was having a look at the two black sleek limousines when some French civilians started coming out of the houses towards us. As they joined us in the doorway I noticed they didn't seem to be acquainted with any of the German soldiers we had taken prisoner, though the Nazis had been living in houses near them. Anyway, they exchanged no greeting as they passed.

As soon as the raid had started the B.B.C. had broadcast to the French and were broadcasting in fact at that moment. The speaker was telling them, 'Frenchmen! This is a raid and not an invasion ... Don't take part in any way that might bring reprisals on the part of the enemy ... We appeal to your coolness and good sense ... When the time comes we will let you know ... It is then that we will act side by side for our common victory and your liberty.'

We'd been given leaflets worded in the same strain to distribute to any French people we encountered. These leaflets were of thin, flimsy paper so they wouldn't be bulky in our already laden uniforms.

We handed them around, and a boy in his teens read his closely and with obvious interest. Then when he was through reading he asked if he might have some more of them. One of the soldiers gave him a pile. He seemed a keen youngster, and we concluded that he wanted to dash off and distribute them to all and sundry in the neighbourhood.

But as he folded the leaflets up and put them in his pocket it dawned on me that his request for more of them had been prompted not by any spread-the-news motive, but by the more prosaic fact of France's dire shortage of toilet paper.

II

By now the Jerries had started pounding us with heavy fire. Mortar shells were exploding round us, and they seemed to be coming mainly from a huge concrete fort that I could discern up on the hilly golf course.

The boom of heavy artillery fire, added to the mortars, the clatter of machine-guns, the *ping* of snipers bullets, and the roar of aircraft that had now appeared overhead, produced a terrific din which was incessant throughout the time we were ashore.

In the midst of all this noise there came another sound that made us fully alive to the homelike atmosphere of our battlefield, which brought suddenly to our minds a picture of what it must have been like for the French people living here to be awakened out of their night's slumber and be confronted with the spectacle of Nazi garrison troops and five thousand Allied visitors fighting out a battle royal in their streets and back gardens. For the Canadian troops the whole thing was a battle, a coming to grips with the enemy. It was part of the picture of their role in this war, something they had trained for and thought about for months, years now. But to the French civilians it was a sudden, unexpected interruption to their daily lives. What brought this home to us with a start was that in the midst of this bombardment of noise we heard a sound we were so familiar with it carried us back suddenly to everyday life – it was the tinkle of some Frenchman's abandoned alarm clock.

Our group of French friends soon dispersed and returned to their homes when it became known to them that Battalion Headquarters was not going to be permanently in the garage and that soon we were going to be moving farther inland. As I watched them return to their homes I couldn't help but feel moved by the way they were taking it all. They kept cool and unflustered. There was no wild stampede to the open country. I didn't see a single Frenchman, throughout the whole six and a half hours I was ashore, heading out of town.

I came away from Dieppe full of admiration for these and the other French people I was to see later later in the day. It was one of my outstanding impressions of the whole operation, the wonderful morale of the French. There they'd been, unarmed civilians, with every type of hell known to modern warfare breaking out around them – from machine-guns to dive-bombers and they'd remained perfectly calm, showed not the slightest sign of panic.

I could also feel assured, without as shadow of doubt, just what the attitude was going to be when the time came to announce, 'Frenchmen! This is not merely a raid, it's the invasion!'

III

From an officer I learned just what specific role the battalion was undertaking in the streets of Pourville and in the surrounding countryside.

The task of our A Company was to go through the valley to a radio-location centre and an anti-aircraft battery and put them out of action. B Company was working in the streets, house-clearing, taking prisoners, and clearing the way for the Canadian Cameron Highlanders to come through. The Camerons were to advance through us. C Company went to work on the right flank, up in the terraces, silencing machine-gun posts and smoothing the way for the Camerons. And D Company had a similar assignment on the left flank.

The operations of the troops in our regiment were conducted by Colonel Merritt and his second-in-command Major McRae. Colonel Merritt had the Command Post and Major McRae Battalion Headquarters, and they were both continually in touch by wireless with the headquarters ship out at sea, from which the whole operation was being run.

Each of these two groups moved about throughout the engagement. They were entirely separate and usually quite far apart, so that if either was put out of action the other could still carry on.

Having landed with Battalion Headquarters I stayed with them for most of the time. For the sake of the uninitiated, I might mention that, though the words 'battalion headquarters' might conjure up a picture of a cluster of desks bestrewn with maps and other papers and peopled by a staff of officers and clerks, it consisted in fact merely of the Major, his Adjutant, and two signallers with their portable wireless. In the garage we were B.H.Q. from the running boards of two laid-up cars.

As well as myself, there was another camp-follower – an official British Army war photographer, Sergeant Holloway. He was employed at that moment in getting a series of pictures of the German prisoners. He was young and had only just been transferred to the army photographic unit. In fact, he confided in me on the way over that this was the first assignment he had gone on. As the day progressed I watched him taking some really outstanding action pictures and then later lost track of him. I heard he'd been injured in an eye but was still carrying on. When we got back to England he was reported as missing.

IV

We didn't stay long in the garage of that house by the promenade, but pushed forward across the grass square and set ourselves up in one corner. We had just got our wireless set going when there was a terrific crash, and a mortar shell exploded in the middle of the square.

I was lying down at the time, but the force of the explosion sent me flying, and I felt what seemed to be pebbles hitting my back, like little stones from a motor car wheel. My ears started ringing, and my head felt as thought it was suspended in mid-air, swinging back and forth like a pendulum.

Out of the corner of my eye I caught a glimpse of a young officer who was standing with his back to the explosion, Spurts of blood shot out from the front part of his neck and shoulder as the shell splinters went right through him. He toppled forward into the arms of a companion.

I didn't think any more about the pebbles that had hit my body, until an hour or so later, when my trousers and shirt began to feel damp. It was a hot, sunny day, and at first I concluded it was merely perspiration. But it was blood, and those 'pebbles' had been shell fragments.

Fortunately, few of our men were casualties from this particular explosion, but four of the German prisoners were killed. As we were coming out I saw their bodies lying there on the grass, stiff and pallid.

Jerry was using his mortars with deadly accuracy now. He was right on to us, and whenever we in Battalion Headquarters moved he followed us with his mortar fire. Naturally B.H.Q. and the Command Post are two of the things that the enemy tries hard to put out of action. They're the nerve centres of a battalion, and if they can be captured or blown up it's going to result in disorganization of the troops. So we were pounded at every spot we established ourselves.

They were probably four-inch mortars the Germans were using. They certainly had a longer range than our own three-inch models, and they were exceedingly hard to spot, either because they were using a smokeless charge or they were sending the shells up from deep pits in the ground. I was to learn from a soldier who'd been through the last war that there was nothing novel about the deadliness of an enemy's mortar fire. They'd developed it to a high pitch of efficiency and effectiveness in the last war too.

It's probably unnecessary to describe what a mortar is and its functions. However, it's a simple sort of weapon, rather like a stove-pipe. The shell is dropped down this pipe, hits a striker at the bottom which sets off the charge in the shell and shoots it out again up into the air. Formerly aiming was just a matter of holding the mortar at a different angle until you struck the one which would lob the shells where you wanted them to go, but nowadays there are much more accurate appliances for aiming.

The mortar is a very useful weapon. It's ideal for when you're at comparatively close range and want to get an objective behind a high building or a similar obstacle. The Germans concentrated mainly on mortar fire for getting at us among the buildings in Dieppe, supporting it with machine-gun and rifle fire.

They were able to be accurate for three reasons.

First of all, it's natural that with their defence arrangements they'd tabulated every point where an invading force would be likely to establish itself once it had landed. For these places they'd have fixed ranges, and it would be just an automatic procedure banging away at them.

Also I noted that where Focke-Wulfs flew down low over us a minute or so later mortar shells would be bursting on top of us, which didn't require much deduction to conclude that they were using observation planes for directing their mortar fire.

And, thirdly, each time we put our wireless sets into action we seemed to get a dose of mortar; Jerry must have been able to range our wireless.

Chapter 7

Colonel Merritt at the Bridge

I

Ijoined some of our men who were advancing along the main street towards the bridge that led to the centre of Dieppe, a mile and a half away. The street was wide and flanked by shops, hotels, and picket-fenced lawns – the typical holiday resort sort of street along which you'd take a pleasant stroll on a summer's evening.

No pleasant stroll was ours this time. The roadway and pavements were being peppered with snipers' bullets, and I could hear them pinging on the concrete and clattering against the fences as I joined in the crouching jog-trot of the troops.

I recall now that I wasn't scared. Time and time again in my work I've interviewed survivors from torpedoed destroyers and other people who've been through similarly harrowing experiences. I'd invariably asked how they felt while it was on, and always the reply would come back: 'I was too busy doing such-and-such to think about being scared.'

Well, here I was having a first-hand close-up experience. I was certainly conscious that I was in danger, but one thing and one thing only was uppermost in my mind as I went along that street. I had to get to the relative security of an alleyway between two buildings next to the bridge, and the quicker I did it the less time I would be a target for the snipers.

I wasn't scared, because I didn't have time to think about it. But later in the day I was to be scared as hell for three solid hours – which I'll tell you about when we come to it.

The alleyway was about twenty yards from the start of the bridge. The bridge was really an aqueduct, some two hundred yards long. It was wide and had no balustrades or cover of any sort, making it very exposed. Towering above it on the other side of the river was the concrete fort. The men formed up in their sections and I watched the first batch go forward across that stretch of exposed concrete roadway about two rugby fields in length.

Jerry at once let loose a shower of concentrated hell on that bridge. Chunks of concrete shot up in the air as mortar shells exploded and a lethal rain of machine-gun bullets pock-marked the smooth surface of the causeway. Many of our men fell, and I dashed out with the stretcher-bearers to help drag back the wounded.

The narrow alleyway became crowded with the injured. Those for whom there weren't stretchers were laid out on the gravel with tin hats as a prop for their heads while the stretcher-bearers went to work applying bandages, slashing away bits of clothing to get at the wounds. I lit cigarettes for those who wanted them, held my water bottle to their lips.

Nobody cried out in pain, though you only needed to look at their gashed bodies to know what they were going through. As they lay there, they'd say, 'Christ my leg,' or 'Take a look at my shoulder,' or grit their teeth and look up at you and say 'Hello, bud.'

The stretcher-bearers did their work with an unhurried calm that gave the injured men the comforting assurance that nobody was going to forget about them and they were going to be taken care of properly no matter what was happening. Someone said, 'Jesus, these boys are doing a swell job.' They did a swell job everywhere, in the streets and on the beaches going out. They went out into anything to get the wounded back into shelter. They manned the stretchers and carried the men along the main street to a clearing-station. Stretcher-bearers ... the R.A.F. ground crews ... there are a lot of people in this war whom the headlines overlook.

Over on the other side of the street, which was strewn with telephone wires dangling from a battered telegraph pole, we could see our troops who had come up to cross the bridge. They were some of the Canadian Camerons and their piper was there with his pipes under his arms. A Winnipeg battalion of the famous Scottish Regiment, they carried on the tradition of going into battle to the skirl of the bagpipes. One of the pipers had the novel experience of having his pipes punctured by a shell-fragment when he had them going at full blast.

One of their men ran across the road and told us about their landing on the beach. They'd come ashore half an hour after us and hadn't enjoyed the unmolested dash up the beach that we had. Jerry had blazed at them as soon as their landing craft hit the beach. They'd lost their colonel. The moment he put his foot on the pebbles a bullet hit him in the centre of his forehead.

II

As the men got ready to tackle the bridge again an officer came walking up the street. It was Colonel Merritt. He stopped and spoke to us, taking his tin hat off and mopping the perspiration from his brow as he did so.

'What's the trouble?' he asked.

'This bridge is a hot spot, sir. We're trying to get across it.'

'Okay. Come with me.'

Merritt walked out into the middle of the street again and said, 'Now, men, we're going to get across the bridge. Follow me. Don't bunch up. Spread out. Here we go!'

And he strode off to the bridge, erect, calm, and determined-looking. He showed no sign of concern at the 'muck' that was flying around him. His tin hat dangled from his wrist, and he twirled it around as he walked. His men followed him as he advanced into the very face of the white concrete fortress on the hill.

Watching this display of bravery and inspired leadership, I felt a thrill run through me. A stretcher-bearer beside me shook his head incredulously and said, 'My God!'

Most of the men got across this time. Merritt himself before the day was through was to cross the bridge no fewer than six times. He was soon leading other men across and saying as he set off, 'Come on over – there's nothing to it.'

How he came through the rain of shells and bullets unscathed heaven alone knows. The last sight of Merritt I got was just before we left Dieppe, and the only sign of injury he had then was a scratch on his nose. He didn't come back with us. He went down on to the beach as the last men were leaving. He made sure they got off safely and then grabbed some Tommy-guns and rifles and headed back into the town. As he went he shouted over his shoulder, 'I'm going to get even with these swine for what they've done to my regiment.'

He set up a final, one-man pocket of resistance to hold up the German reinforcements who were heading down towards the beach to get at the men who were coming away.

Throughout the whole operation Merritt displayed just plain, unvarnished bravery. I'd never seen anything like it in my life, and perhaps will never see it again. What makes bravery like that? I don't know what it is. It's something that comes from inside. Merritt had that inner calm, a realization that you're guided by God, and when death comes, if it's to come perhaps suddenly and long before you have lived your allotted span, you accept that.

Merritt had such an utter disregard for his own welfare. He was prepared in the end to die fighting. Just exactly what he did after those of us who came back had left the beach. The next thing we heard was he had been taken prisoner. In a prison camp in Germany he learned that he had been awarded the Victoria Cross.

III

The courage Colonel Merritt displayed was no isolated act of heroism at Dieppe.

There was Charlie Sawden.

I met Sawden on the transport ship leaving England, He was one of a group I chatted with as they were fusing hand-grenades. I was asking some of the boys what part of Saskatchewan they came from and what their jobs had been in civilian life. I figured out in the heat of battle there wasn't going to be much time to go round with my notebook interviewing some Canadian in the midst of a hand-to-hand encounter with a German in the act of storming a pill-box. So I was getting some of the 'spade-work' of the reporting done on the ship going over.

A Fortunate Survivor

Canadian war correspondent Wallace Reyburn, flanked by British Army photographer Lieutenant David Lockyear (*left*) and Quentin Reynolds of *Collier's Weekly*, returning to England after the Dieppe Raid. (*Image from* Rehearsal for Invasion, *1943*)

Wallace Reyburn (*centre*) talking to South Saskatchewan Regiment officers Lt John Edmondson, Major James MacRae, Lt L. Ross MacIlveen and Lt G. B. 'Buck' Buchanan at Toat Hill Camp near Pulborough, Sussex, after they all survived the Dieppe Raid. (*Picture courtesy of the Canadian War Museum*)

A North American B-25 Mitchell bomber flies near Mount Vesuvius during its last eruption in March 1944. At ground level, Reyburn escaped unhurt in a Canadian army jeep. (*Wikimedia Commons*)

Wallace Reyburn astride a donkey mixing with the locals in eastern Europe in the later stage of the war. (*Ross Reyburn*)

Canadian war correspondent Wallace Reyburn in later war years. (*Ross Reyburn*)

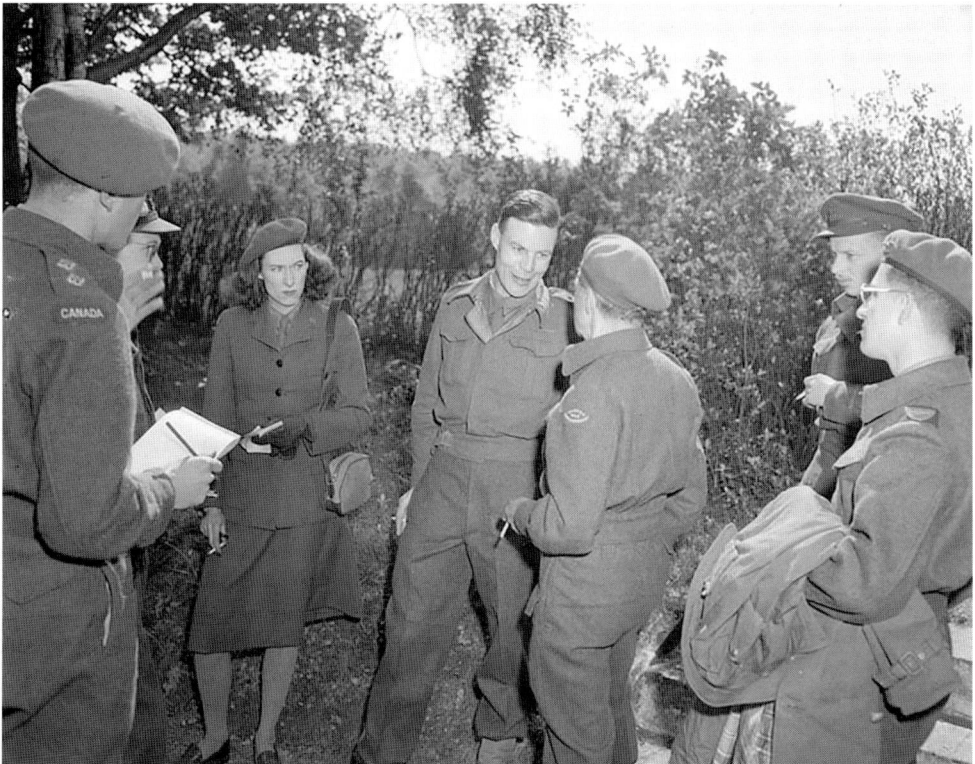

Wallace Reyburn's future wife Betty Munro alongside Lt Col Ces Merritt, VC, when he met the press at the No. 1 Canadian Reception Depot for repatriated prisoners of war at Crookham, England on 21 April 1945. (*A. L. Cole, Library and Archives Canada PA-161938*)

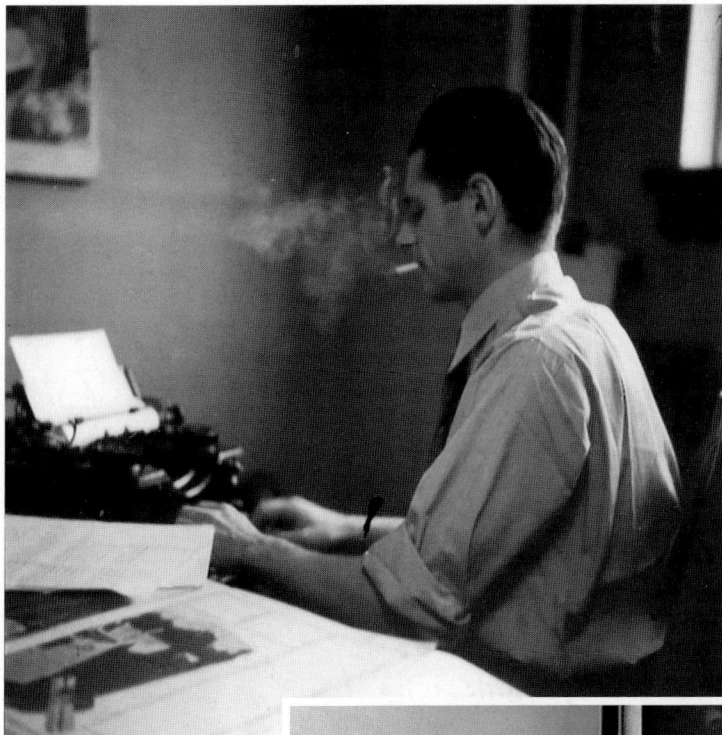

Wallace Reyburn at work. (*Ross Reyburn*)

Wallace Reyburn in the early post-war years as editor of the Toronto-based *New Liberty* magazine. (*Ross Reyburn*)

Reyburn returns to the Dieppe shoreline in 1962, twenty years after he was alongside the first troops clambering ashore in the raid. (*Ross Reyburn*)

Reyburn (third from right back) pictured alongside fellow guest Rolling Stones singer Mick Jagger in a publishing hospitality box at a Lord's Test match. (*Ross Reyburn*)

Wallace Reyburn in later life at his north-west London home. (*Ross Reyburn*)

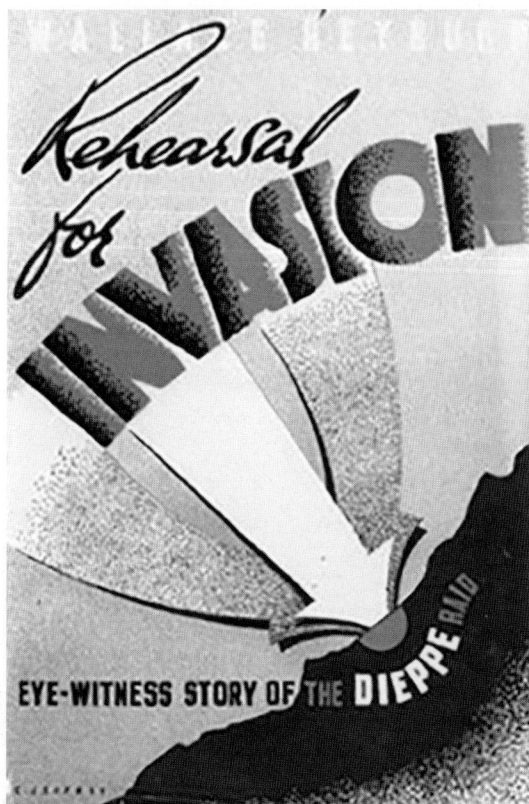

The first edition cover of Wallace Reyburn's eye-witness account the Dieppe Raid, *Rehearsal for Invasion*, published by George G. Harrap & Co. Ltd in 1943.

The Dieppe Raid

Lord Mountbatten, architect of the Dieppe Raid. (*Wikimedia Commons*)

Canadian commander Major General John Hamilton 'Ham' Roberts, who led the operation. (*Canada Dept. of National Defence/Library and Archives Canada/PA-153531*)

Final training exercise prior to assault landing at Dieppe – Canadian infantrymen embark on landing craft. (*Canada Dept. of National Defence/Library and Archives Canada*)

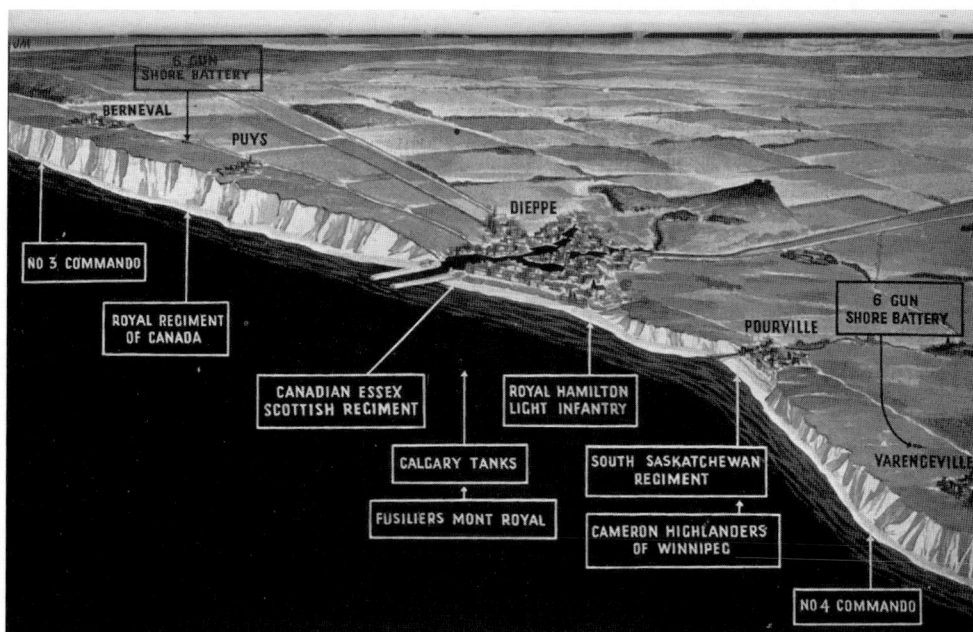

Pictorial map showing Dieppe Raid attack points. (*From* Rehearsal for Invasion, *1943*)

Landing craft en route to Dieppe, France, during Operation Jubilee on 19 August 1942. (*Canada Department of National Defence/Library and Archives Canada/PA-171080*)

Dieppe shoreline viewed from a landing craft as it approaches; fires are burning visibly in the hinterland as a result of the naval and aerial bombardment, by war office official photographer, Lt W. T. Lockyear. (*Wikimedia Commons*)

A German MG34 medium machine-gun emplacement shows the formidable firepower facing Allied troops in the Dieppe Raid. (*Bundesarchiv Bld 1011-291-1213- 34/CC*)

Headquarters destroyer HMS *Calpe* lays a smokescreen off Dieppe. (*Canada Dept. of National Defence/ Library and Archives Canada/LAC PA-116291*)

Three inspirational Dieppe heroes. *Left*: Scottish aristocrat Lord Lovat, with his trademark hunting rifle over his left shoulder and *middle*: Lt Col Ces Merritt, Canada's first VC of the war and *right*: a striking poster of Lt Col Dollard Ménard, awarded the DSO for his extraordinary courage leading the French-Canadian Les Fusiliers Mont-Royal regiment during a doomed attack. (*Wikimedia Commons*)

The aftermath of a disaster. A burning LCT (landing craft tank), abandoned Churchill tanks and the bodies of Allied serviceman on Dieppe's main beach. (*Wikimedia Commons*)

A suicidal mission. A German soldier stands by the bodies of the Royals slaughtered by the sea wall at Puys. (*Wikimedia Commons*)

Captured Canadian soldiers being marched through Dieppe. (*Canada Department of National Defence/Library and Archives Canada/LAC-PA200058*).

The victors survey the wreckage and dead on Dieppe's main beach. (*Wikimedia Commons*)

German soldiers examine a Churchill tank of the Calgary Tank Regiment, abandoned in the raid. (*Wikimedia Commons*)

The waterfront at Dieppe, France, following the Allied raid. A knocked-out Churchill tank is visible in the centre. (*Wikimedia Commons*)

An unidentified Canadian soldier, armed with a Thompson sub-machine gun, escorts a German prisoner captured during Operation Jubilee. (*Canada Dept. of National Defence/ Library and Archives Canada/PA– 210156*)

Exhausted Canadian soldiers return from Dieppe, 19 August 1942. (*Lt Spender, War Office Official Photographer, LAC PA-183775*)

British commandos returning to Newhaven in their landing craft. (*Lt Spender, War Office Official Photographer, Wikimedia Commons*)

Captains E. L. McGivern and J. H. Medhurst examine a German pillbox at Dieppe, 3 September 1944, two years after the Royal Regiment of Canada soldiers were slaughtered on the beach below. (*Canada Department of National Defence/ Library and Archives Canada/ LAC PA-134448*)

The triumphant return. Canadian soldiers marching through liberated Dieppe on 1 September 1944. (*LAC/PA-1231233*)

Sawden is a short, stockily built fellow, with close-cropped hair above a weather-beaten face which is frequently enlightened by a broad grin. He comes from a small town called Consul, out on the Saskatchewan prairies. About his pre-war career I found him inclined to be reticent. He grinned, 'Just put me down as a "horse thief" and let it go at that.'

Sawden was one of a section that penetrated well behind the town, and at one point they were held up by a pill-box. It was surrounded by a sea of closely meshed barbed wire, and from its apertures came a withering spray of machine-gun bullets.

The men took shelter and debated their best plan of action. Eventually Sawden announced, 'I'll fix those guys in there.'

He strapped a bayonet to each trouser leg and loaded himself up with hand-grenades. He told his companions to wait where they were. They held their breath as they watched him walk out from cover and advance on the pill-box, still spitting out its barrage of machine-gun fire.

Once in striking distance, Sawden took aim and then flung his grenades through the windows. The seven Nazis inside were blown to bits, and our men found what was left of their bodies when they took over the strong-point. Sawden is walking about England to-day without a scratch on him – and he's ready, he'll tell you, to do the same thing again any time the need may arise.

IV

And there was the French-Canadian named Pierre Dubuc, of the Fusiliers Mont Royal, whom with some other men got well into the central part of Dieppe. They were captured. Their clothes were taken off them, the Germans figuring that would prevent them trying to escape. Clad only in their undershorts, they were taken to a stone wall and told to face it. A youthful Nazi machine-gunner was left to guard them while the N.C.O. and the other soldier went into a near-by building that was some sort of headquarters.

Dubuc did some quick thinking. He turned to the young Nazi and asked, 'Do you speak English?'

The German said, 'A little.'

'How about a glass of water?' asked Dubuc, passing a signal down the row of colleagues lined up against the wall.

The Nazi turned his head away for a moment to see where the nearest water was, and as he did so the Canadians pounced on him. One of the men seized a length of iron piping that was lying one the ground and bashed the guard's head in.

They dashed off to the beach and found the colonel of their regiment lying there wounded. Dubuc lifted him up on to his shoulders and carried him across the inferno of shell and machine-gun fire of the beach to one of the barges.

It was from one of those barges, as it was heading away from Dieppe, that an Army padre jumped overboard into the shallow waters and swam back up into the town. As he went he called out, 'There are lots of padres to look after the men in England. Those men ashore need me.'

Chapter 8

The Air Battle

I

I'd often heard old soldiers remark that in ten minutes under actual fire you learn more about how to take cover and such things than you can learn in months of training. I soon found out how true this was.

I'd no military grooming for this episode. I'd come straight from my office desk. But there are a few things so elementary about taking shelter from a barrage that you find yourself doing the right thing instinctively. I soon discovered the best type of cover to seek from mortar shells.

By now they were dropping round us more plentifully. But I noticed that when one shot the top of hotel or large house it merely blew a chunk off the top storey, and its explosion wasn't heavy enough to demolish the whole building. There is no warning screech or whine to a mortar shell, such as that that precedes an artillery shell or bomb.

You are conscious merely of a series of sharp, ear-splitting crashes going on about you as the shells are lobbed into your midst. Most of the mortar fire seemed to be coming from the fort up on the golf course and from other points in that direction, so when I decided to take time out to watch the dog-fights that were going on overhead – the sky was full of aircraft now – I took up a position against the side of a three-storey house, on the side away from the spot whence most of the shells were coming.

Another thing I realized was the explosion of a mortar shell throws the metal splinters upward and outward, and though a shell might go off on the ground close to you, if you are low enough down the fragments would fly harmlessly over your head.

So I had an ideal place because where I was sitting the ground sloped away from the street, and though one mortar shell did hit the roof above me and several landed on the street not many yards away, nothing hit me, and as I sat watching the planes fighting it out I felt quite secure from the enemy's barrage and was, in fact, complimenting myself on getting the thing figured out. A little later I was to have a rude awakening, however. My observation post turned out to be not quite the haven I thought it was.

As I looked up at the planes overhead I saw the first Nazi aircraft I'd seen in flight. Since coming to Europe I'd seen relics of German planes that had been brought down in England. During the Blitzes on London I'd heard the drone of bombers overhead, but never been able to see one. I'd built up a yen inside me actually to set eyes on the enemy aircraft that did the bomb-dropping and fought it out with our fighter planes. Now I saw not one. But dozens of them.

I had a queer sort of sensation out of it, akin to seeing in the flesh a celebrity I'd seen many times in photographs. Most of the aircraft were Focke-Wulfs and there's no doubt about the fact that in flight it's a beautiful-looking plane. These ones were painted a creamy silver colour, and they glinted in the sunlight as they swooped and spiralled above us, with a deep blue sky as background. I sensed right then the thrill of pride the Germans must get when they see these fighter planes careering about the sky. But it must be rather galling for them to have to confront themselves with the solid truth that the world's No. 1 fighter plane is still the Spitfire.

The aerial battle that was going on all the time we were ashore and coming away from Dieppe was the biggest that had been fought in Western Europe since the Battle of Britain. For months before the R.A.F. and squadrons of other Allied forces based in Britain had been going out on sweeps over Northern France and the Low Countries, trying to entice the Luftwaffe into the air for a fight. But the Germans weren't having any of it. All that ever resulted from those sweeps were minor aerial skirmishes, never anything on a big scale, because Germany was bent on conserving her western-based aircraft, depleted as they were by the needs of the Russian front.

But at Dieppe the Luftwaffe had to come up. Not only did they put everything into the sky that they had available in the aerodromes of Northern France, but they brought reinforcements from Belgium and even as far afield as Holland.

In England, to provide the absolute maximum air umbrella to cover the British troops on the ground and the flotilla of transport ships and escort vessels, squadrons of Fighter, Bomber, Coastal and Army Co-operation Commands were brought down from stations in the north of England to augment those operating from airfields in the south. Each of those aerodromes was the terminus of a cross-Channel shuttle service that went on at a hectic pace throughout the day, from dawn until far into the night.

Our bombers were directed at such key points behind Dieppe at Abbeville and Rouen. Their job was to disrupt transport by bombing road junctions, railways lines, and stations, to hinder the enemy in bringing up land reinforcements. Our fighter plans were to intercept German bombers and fighters as they took off from their flying-fields, to shoot them down if possible before they could get over to Dieppe.

There was no heavy bombing of Dieppe itself before we landed. After the raid there was much criticism on this score. It was held that our air power was used purely defensively, not offensively. Some critics have said that bombers should have gone in before we landed and blasted hell out of the coastal forts and batteries, softened the place up for us. But if that had been done any element of surprise we might have hoped to have would have been nullified.

An air raid on Dieppe just before we landed would have awakened all the Nazi troops in the garrisons, at the anti-aircraft posts, on the shore batteries. They'd have been up and about on the alert. The reinforcements inland would have been given a hint right away that something was afoot and would have been rushed to the coast. We should have arrived to find the enemy sitting waiting for us along the whole stretch of the coastline.

Those who planned the raid were faced with the choice of two modes of opening the attack. First, they could have sent in an advance bombing force to bomb the forts and shore batteries so heavily that a sufficient number would be put out of action so effectively they would be unable to oppose our landings. Or secondly, they could use the element of surprise, doing the silencing of shore batteries by the use of Commandos employing sneak methods.

The planners chose the second method. As it transpired, things did not turn out well. The element of surprise was lost on the left flank, and the shore batteries in that region were never put out of action. By then, however, it was too late to bring in the bombers. Our men were ashore, and it would have been a matter of killing our own troops.

Another way in which air power could have been used offensively at Dieppe, other critics have said, would have been to make use of paratroops and other airborne troops. The Dieppe operation was purely a frontal attack. No attempt was made to get at the enemy from behind. I have dealt with this matter earlier in the book.

Nevertheless, when the air aspect of Dieppe is judged objectively, merely as a battle between two opposing air forces, it's abundantly clear that the R.A.F. gave the Luftwaffe a sound drubbing. A hundred and seventy Axis planes have definitely been confirmed as shot down, and many others were damaged. We lost a hundred and six.

II

As I sat against the wall of the house watching the planes overhead I became conscious of a sound that at first puzzled me. It was faint but persistent. After a while I began wondering what it was. Then I realized that it was the sound of voices. There were people inside the house, in the cellar, moving about and talking.

Since my first meeting with the French people earlier in the morning I'd almost forgotten about them, but, looking about now, I noticed several of them at their windows.

From where I was sitting I could look down the long valley behind the town. On that flat riverside land there were several farms, and near the barn of one of these, about a quarter of a mile away, I caught sight of a farmer moving about. I watched him stroll about his meadow, pause every now and then, and look up at the planes flying by. He seemed quite unaware that the fort on the golf course was firing mortar shells directly over his head at the terraces on the other side of the valley, where detachments of our men had now penetrated.

I saw him bring his four cows into the relative shelter of the barn and then stroll across the meadow to bring in a pile of hay for them.

The determination to carry on business as usual, come what may, was shared by another Frenchman we encountered. An aged fellow, wearing no hat and without a shirt under his jacket, he apparently had his mind set on having fresh bread for his meals that day. He was cycling along a street on his bicycle. Either he reasoned that the Nazi snipers would recognize his civilian status or else he had a profound disregard for the likelihood of being dispatched by a chunk of flying metal – anyway, he was pedalling along gaily, a long French loaf propped up in the basket on the front of his bike.

Most of the French women were staying indoors, down in their cellars for shelter or watching from their windows. But there was a decided inclination of the part of the men, and particularly boys, to be out and about and to get a good view of what was going on.

There was a little French boy who probably got a bigger kick out of the raid than any of us. He was only about eight or nine. He was wearing a grey shirt and knickerbockers and a bright blue beret. He evinced great interest in our activities, watched our men firing mortars, asked them all sorts of questions about how the weapons worked. He was fascinated by our signallers and their portable wireless sets. He dashed hither and thither among our troops, keeping in touch with every phase of the battle.

I caught sight of him now, across the other side of the square opposite to where I was. As well as being a keen student of modern war, he also seemed to be well informed as to battle tactics of a former era. He wanted to get across the street, so he drew on his knowledge of the way the settlers out West in the frontier days had matched their wits with the Indians. I watched him crouch behind a house and take his beret off and project it on the end of a stick around the edge of the building.

No sniper took a pot-shot at it, so he concluded the coast was clear. He put his beret back on and dashed across the street.

III

I was joined in a minute or two by an officer.

'Those goddam snipers!' he said, as he paused to regain his breath after his run along the main section of the main road that was getting particular attention from the enemy's snipers.

As we started talking I happened to look over his shoulder towards the houses and buildings up on the wooded terrace. On the veranda of the big white Albion Hotel I noticed somebody moving about.

I said, 'Look out! There's a sniper up there right now.'

'Where?'

I pointed to the hotel, which was about half a mile away from us.

The officer looked through his binoculars and burst into a grin. He handed me the glasses. 'Here,' he said, 'have a look at your sniper.'

He turned out to be a rotund, round-faced Frenchman, with a big moustache and a beret perched on the top of his head. He was strolling up and down the veranda, not the least bit concerned about the commotion that was going on around him. The building a couple of blocks away from his was on fire, and part of the roof of his own hotel had been blown away by a shell. But he was walking blithely back and forth and seemed pleased no end at the wonderful ringside box he had.

My companion soon pushed on, and it wasn't long before I had left that spot too. I made quite an abrupt decision to move on. I'd been complimenting myself on my secluded post, and what seemed quite a safe observation post, and was prepared to stay there some time longer, when I was suddenly brought down to earth by a pinging sound, followed closely by the plonk of a bullet hitting the brickwork beside my head and ricocheting off. A sniper somewhere had spotted me. I lay face downward on the grass and hoped that his aim wouldn't get any better.

I lodged myself in as close as I possibly could to the side of the house and as flat on the ground as I could manage, and went into a hasty conference with myself as to where I'd head for. Along this main street, which ran parallel to the beach and which I'd come along earlier, troops were moving in both directions. First of all one man would go dashing past in the direction of the bridge. Then another would flash by, equally as eager to go in the other direction. All the men who passed seemed to have quite clear in their minds what they were doing, but I was at a loss to fathom who was going where and why.

That's one of the confusing things about street fighting, and many other aspects of modern warfare, for that matter. Everything happens so quickly and in so many places at once that it's hard to keep track of what exactly is going on. I envied the war correspondents of a former day. In the time of the Napoleonic wars, for instance, one could stand on a hill and see two armies ranged against each other in the valley below. Army A would charge, Army B would knock the stuffing out of them, and the war correspondent wound then dash off a thousand-word power piece for his paper. It must have been as easy as reporting Arsenal v Chelsea from the Press box at Wembley.

The difficulty in knowing what the score is while the battle is on is equally a problem for official Army photographers. Though a battle would seem to be a wonderful subject for a photographer, it's far from that. It's a good subject all right – but how to photograph it? Two essential Army tactics – camouflage and dispersal – militate against a cameraman getting good shots. Camouflage nets and the like are designed to make equipment and troops blend in with their surroundings. Photograph them, and you find that they do just that.

Troops don't advance in a neat photographic bunch. They often do in photographs in the Press showing them training. But that's merely a concession granted by their commanding officer at the request of the photographer so that it will 'make a picture'. On the actual battle-field troops are so widely spread out that there's no lens made that will take them all in and make it look a worthwhile shot.

The men who ride in Bren-gun carriers and tanks don't stand up or sit on the turrets, where you can get a good snap of them. They're down out of sight of the enemy – and the photographer. So when he takes a picture of a tank full of men, speeding across the countryside, what does it look like? It looks like an empty tank parked in the open.

Artillery shells and bombs bursting makes a swell picture – if only there was some way of arranging with the enemy to let your photographer know when and where the missiles are going to land, so that he can have his camera set up and focused on the proceedings. Otherwise, it's purely luck when a photographer catches an explosion – and if he's close enough to get a really good picture of it, well, he definitely catches the explosion. The best war-time shots that are taken, unfortunately enough, are usually those that are such close-ups that photographer, camera, and film fail to survive.

IV

As I lay beside the house planning my next move I was conscious that I'd better hurry up and get on to that street and join the batches of troops going one of the two ways at their disposal. That sniper was probably at that moment taking another bead at me. I was in a sort of suspended state of anticipation of the next *ping*, and an old and familiar joke flashed into my mind. It was that one about the invalid in a boarding-house who was so sick that the landlady asked the man in the room next to him to make sure that he made no noise as he went to bed at night. The man came home that night and started to go to bed. As he took off one of his boots and dropped it on the floor he heard a groan from the invalid next door and remembered the landlady's request for silence. So when he took off the other boot he placed on gently on the floor, without a sound. He got into bed and went to sleep. At three o'clock in the morning there was a pounding on the wall, and he heard the voice of the invalid. 'For god's sake,' he hollered, 'drop that other boot!' My every sense was attuned to the sniper dropping that other boot.

His next shot, and the last he ever had at me, was lousy – a good two feet above my rump. Nevertheless I decided to make myself a moving target instead of a stationary one, got out onto the road, and joined a couple of soldiers who were headed towards the terraced hill on the west bank of the river. A couple of hundred yards along the road we stopped at what looked and smelled like a stable.

There were several of our men inside. One of them was a little tough-looking sergeant, whose name I learned was Howard Graham. The tunic of his battle-dress was bulging with incendiary bombs, and held another two in his hands. A Sten gun was slung over his shoulder. He was getting ready to go out into the street, and I asked him what he was going to do.

He pointed to one of the streets branching off the main road. 'See that street there,' he said. 'There is a goddam sniper along there who's picking our boys off. I'm going to smoke him out. I'll go along the road setting each house on fire until I get him or he gets me. He'll come running out of doors, and I'll pick him off with this Sten gun.'

There was a determined set to his jaw. He undid another button of his tunic so that he could get at his incendiaries more easily and checked his Sten to see that he had a full magazine. Then he said, 'So long boys,' and headed off along the street.

I didn't see Graham until a couple of hours later. It was when we were making for the beach. He recognized me and said, 'Oh, by the way, newspaperman, I got that sniper all right.'

Chapter 9

Germans versus Canadian Cold Steel

I

I left the stables to work around the houses on the slopes to the west of the town. The place was starting to look a wreck. Long strands of telephone wire were dangling on the ground. There didn't seem to be a single building that hadn't had some part blown away. The roadway was littered with rubble, and there were tin hats and rifles and other pieces of equipment lying about. As I went along the road a shell hit the top of a tree a couple of hundred yards ahead of me and showers of leaves fluttered down on to the pavement through the fumes of the explosion.

I came up to a corporal and a private bringing in four Nazis. The Canadians had their helmets tipped on the back of their heads, and their faces were grimy and sweaty.

The corporal wiped the perspiration from his forehead with the back of his sleeve and said, 'God, it's hot.' He nodded towards the four Germans. 'Here's another batch for the collection.'

I asked them if they spoke English, but they shook their heads in silence.

'No, they can't speak English,' said the corporal sarcastically.

'All they can say is Kamerad.

'Y' know,' he went on, 'these Nazis are yellow when it comes to a real fight. You see these four guys. Well, they had a machine-gun nest in the woods up there. They were giving us hell. So we decided to storm the place. We headed straight up the hill with our bayonets. Right in the open. We hadn't got half-way up when they came running out with their hands over their heads and shouting 'Kamerad.'

Here was that old one again – 'the Germans can't bear the sight of cold steel.' I turned to the other Canadian to hear his version. He nodded his head. 'That's right,' he said. 'These bastards haven't got the guts when it comes to a hand-to-hand fight. They're like a lot of cheap gangsters. Take their weapons away from them and they're yellow.'

He and his companion didn't conceal their disgust and, looking them over, they both looked the type who could dish it out.

I watched them go further off down the road with their prisoners and then went further up into the woods. I met there with other men who had been fighting with the enemy at close quarters. They all had stories to tell of groups of the Germans throwing in the sponge when the likelihood of a hand-to-hand fight loomed up.

I talked to a half-caste Indian named Huppe. He'd spent most of his life in the backwoods of Canada as a hunter and trapper and had become an outstanding rifle-shot. Just before I arrived he'd picked off ten Germans in the space of half an hour or so.

Huppe's views about the Germans as fighting men were, 'They're all right when they're sitting behind their machine-guns in their forts, and you're down below them in the open, and they can shower you with bullets from the safety of their pill-boxes. But get up close to them and they fold up.'

II

This legend of the Germans' dislike for cold steel started in the last war and has been accepted generally ever since. There's no doubt about the fact that some of the German soldiers we came up against at Dieppe preferred saving their own skins and becoming prisoners of war to fighting it out with bayonets. But to generalize from that that all the Nazis hadn't any guts is both inaccurate and dangerous. Any army without fighting spirit could not have achieved all that the German army achieved so far in this war. They're formidable fighters equipped with very efficient weapons – one only has to look at the record to realize that. To minimize your enemy is to go into battle with false confidence.

But it wasn't over-confidence that the Canadians got from these displays of gutlessness by many of the German garrison troops they came across. It was more a feeling of frustration.

The Canadians in the last war had a reputation for being tough fighters. This war's Canadians in their training in England had shown every evidence of being as solid a proposition as their forerunners in 1914–18. We war correspondents who had been covering their training for months now had sent back to the Dominion countless articles with such titles as 'McNaughton's Men are Tough' and had meant every word of it.

At Dieppe they were on test. They were spoiling for a real fight after months and months of mock battles. As they came ashore and got in among the streets there was a 'let-me-get-at-'em' attitude about every one of them. It was an eagerness to mix it with the enemy that stemmed partly from their long period of inactivity, their waiting for zero hour, and partly from the fact that they wanted to prove to the world that they were very bit as good as the Canadians who had done so outstandingly in the last war.

Also, the Australians and the New Zealanders and other Dominion soldiers had seen action on various battlefields. The Canadians were the only Dominion troops that hadn't as yet been in a major operation. They wanted to show that that had been no fault of theirs, that they wanted to fight as much as anyone else did.

So they'd arrived on the scene rarin' to go. They tackled the thing like wildcats. But they were soon to find out that they were fighting in a battle in which most of the cards were stacked against them.

They had to assail a firmly entrenched enemy in giant forts and strongly fortified pill-boxes. That in itself didn't mean they were at a hopeless disadvantage. What did weigh the balance heavily in favour of the enemy was the fact that the Canadians were fighting with light weapons against very heavy stuff. As I stood watching the battle in the sector I was located in I would hear the heavy boom of the German artillery, the explosions of their mortars. In reply would come the *ping* of Canadian rifle fire, the *rat-a-tat* of mere Bren guns and Stens. It seemed like answering a cannon with a pop-gun.

No artillery was landed with the raiding force. Those who planned the raid had no doubt reasoned that being a raiding force, which was going to strike deep and depart, heavy weapons such as artillery would be too cumbersome. Thus the troops were restricted to light arms, weapons the men could carry themselves. Only in the central sector were they supported ashore by anything heavier than their infantry weapons, that was by the guns of the tanks. Even machine-guns weren't included, except for a small number of them on the centre beach.

What artillery fire was provided came from naval vessels out at sea, but this was not nearly as effective as howitzers would have been, had it been possible to land them and bring them into action against the enemy's strong-points, as is done in a normal land operation.

In other words, the Canadians were tackling with light infantry weapons strongly fortified points that had not been softened up beforehand by an effective artillery barrage or bombing.

But they went at their job with a fervour and spirit that knew no bounds. We learned a lot at Dieppe. The Germans learned something too – they learned that when they are up against the Canadians they are up against fighters with a capital F.

Chapter 10

The Withdrawal Starts

I

By ten o'clock we were ready to leave. Our dead and wounded were being taken down to an empty building on the promenade. Battalion Headquarters had been set up in a house about fifty yards inland from it. Colonel Merritt wirelessed to the headquarters ship, lying a few miles out to sea, saying that we were ready to leave and asking for the landing craft to be sent in for us. The reply came back that they'd be into the beach for us at eleven. That delay couldn't be avoided. It would take the boats that long to get in.

Several companies of the South Saskatchewans and the Winnipeg Camerons were fighting a rearguard action, holding up the German reinforcements that were now coming up in force to try and catch us before we got off. They were coming down the wooded slope behind us and the overflow of their rifle and machine-gun fire, directed at our men who were fighting back, started to penetrate us. Bullets commenced splattering on the roof of our house. We couldn't see them in the woods there, but they were now so close that it became obvious that it was going to be a toss-up who reached us first – our boats or the Nazis.

There were several hundred men concentrated in those few blocks of buildings adjoining the promenade. The Nazi troops in the forts and at the artillery guns farther back inland knew we were there and were directing everything on to us. Focke-Wulf 190s and Messerschmitts swooped down over us, and they came so low that you felt you could reach out and touch them. You could see the tips of their cannon and machine-guns blaze red as they peppered us with cannon shells and bullets. I watched our men go out into the streets and squares under these swooping planes and blast up at them with their rifles and Sten guns.

Colonel Merritt was directing operations from a gravel pathway which ran alongside the house in which Battalion Headquarters had been set up. His signallers were at work at their wireless sets and were standing up against the scanty shelter of a high stone wall. Merritt was bare-headed, his tin hat hanging from his wrist. As the enemy planes came down over us he didn't as much as duck. Standing perfectly erect, he'd look at them as they flashed by.

It might have seemed a foolhardy thing for Merritt to do to stand out there in the open with mortar shells and artillery shells dropping all around us and those enemy fighter planes coming down at us, but he was out there for the very good reason that he wanted to have a clear view of what was going on, so that he'd be able to direct operations properly.

We looked out to sea, and there was still no sign of the boats. The German troops behind us were getting closer now. We knew that, because their bullets were now splattering on the upper storey of the house.

II

I stood in the doorway and watched our stretcher-bearers carrying wounded down to the promenade. Colonel Merritt debated with his officer what should be done about the dozens of prisoners we'd taken. It looked as though we were going to have a tough enough job getting our dead and wounded and ourselves off the beach without the trouble of taking Germans along. So it was decided that when we left we'd just leave them there.

None of the prisoners that the South Saskatchewans or Winnipeg Camerons took were bound. After Dieppe the Germans claimed that instructions had been given by our commanding officers to bind the hands of prisoners behind their backs so that they couldn't get at their papers and destroy them. This alleged order prompted the Germans to manacle Canadian and British prisoners taken at Dieppe. Britain and Canada replied by manacling a like number of Germans prisoners among those held in the United Kingdom and Canada.

If such an order to bind prisoners had actually been given at Dieppe there is no evidence that it would have violated the international agreement on the treatment of prisoners in the field. Binding a prisoner during a battle is quite a different matter from manacling him in a prison camp. There is no clause in the agreement that the former should not be done, but the latter definitely does violate the rules set down.

In today's fast-moving warfare, of which hit-and-run raids such as Dieppe are such a feature, prisoners present a real problem. In static trench warfare prisoners can always be moved back behind the lines for safe-keeping. But every minute we were at Dieppe prisoners were a hazard. They had to be watched closely, for they'd snap at every opportunity to turn the tables on their guards. Abandoned hand-grenades, rifles and revolvers were lying about all over the place – there was no time in the heat of battle for someone to go round collecting them up, and a prisoner only had to wait his chance to grab one of these while a guard happened to be looking the other way. Things like that did actually happen at Dieppe. One officer I talked with after the raid told me how he saved his life in the nick of time. He was standing near a group of prisoners when a sound behind him made him turn quickly. He was just in time to see a German prisoner taking a bead on him with a rifle. In Wild West style he fired his revolver from the hip, and, luckily for him, he was quicker on the trigger than the German.

Far from the Canadians ill-treating prisoners that were taken, quite the opposite seemed to be the case. I remember when the first prisoners were being lined up for examination a couple of privates were going through their pockets, taking out pocket-books, papers, combs, and so on, and placing them in a pile on the ground. As soon as he saw what they were doing an officer reprimanded them.

'Don't put their belongings in all in one pile,' he said. 'You'll mix up the money and when we've left these poor guys will have a helluva fight deciding what belongs to who. Put the things in separate piles.'

III

The minutes crept by, and the hands of our watches moved with the slowness of a watched kettle coming to the boil. Would they never get round to eleven o'clock. We looked out to sea, and it was empty and bare. No signs of the boats yet.

A spray of machine-gun pellets splattered across the side of the house, a few feet above my head indicated that the Germans were getting nearer. It meant they were down in the valley now. I started wondering what it would be like to be a prisoner of war.

Then a shout went up. The boats had been sighted.

Earlier in the morning I'd found a German tin hat lying on the ground. I still had it with me and figured on taking it back as a souvenir. But now that we were going to head for the beach it struck me that this tin hat might be quite useful. As we were going to head down to the beach the enemy's fire would be coming from behind us, so why not use the tin hat as a bit of rear protection. I strapped it to my water-bottle and with a piece of string attached it firmly to my waist so that is sat securely on my behind.

As I did this my mind flashed back to a Canadian air-gunner I'd once talked to after he got back from a raid on Germany. He was a rear-gunner in a Halifax. Those aircraft are so big and roomy that the air crews invariably wear tins hats as protection against ack-ack and enemy fighter planes' fire. As he'd got out of the plane he'd had his tin hat in hand, and I asked him if he'd worn it throughout the raid. 'Sure I wore it,' he said, 'but not on my head. My guess was that if I was going to be hit it would be by ack-ack coming up from under me. So I sat on my tin hat.'

The wounded were taken off first. Then the Colonel signalled a hundred men to go down to the boats. I was among the next batch to go down.

As we set off along the road to the promenade I heard Merritt's voice. 'Don't run men,' he shouted. 'Slope arms and march to the beach.'

I saw the man in front of me shoulder his rifle and start marching. I'd been dashing forward in a crouching position, hoping that that way

I'd be less of a target for the snipers, but I automatically raised myself erect and marched with the men around me.

The wide concrete promenade was strewn with bodies. I stepped over the body of a Canadian soldier lying face downward in a pool of blood. I caught a glimpse of another man lying on his back. The whole of the front part of his clothing had been torn away, probably by an explosion. His exposed body was a bright yellow colour. Why yellow? I remember wondering what caused that.

When I reached the edge of the promenade I notice a ladder leaning against the twelve-foot parapet. At the foot of the ladder, on the beach, was a pile of bodies. The thought flashed through my mind that this ladder was a sort of bottleneck: as the troops came down to the beach they converged on it, because it was the easiest way to get down off the promenade. The sight of that heap of khaki-clad bodies at the foot of it told me that somewhere the Germans had a batch of machine-guns trained on this point.

So I jumped straight down onto the beach.

It wasn't sandy at this part. It was pebble and rock. Thinking back on that jump, I wonder now how I could jump down from height of twelve feet, landing on stones, and come out without so much as a bruise. In my normal senses I'd think twice about jumping that height on to merely grass, but you do that sort of thing in the heat of battle without even thinking about it. A few minutes later in one of the barges I was to do something even crazier and still suffer no ill-effects.

IV

I paused a moment there under the parapet and looked out across the beach.

The tide was full out. Apart from fifty yards or so of pebbles up at the top of the beach it was flat and sandy. It was about three hundred yards from where I was standing to the water's edge. You couldn't see very far out to sea because of the smoke-screen our ships had laid and the hazy smoke from the burning buildings of Dieppe. A haze hung over the whole scene. It was hot and steamy, and there was the dank heavy odour in your nostrils of seaweed, salt water and blood.

The beach was dotted with prone figures on the sand and men running out to the boats. There were boats with their noses grounded on the sand every hundred yards or so along the whole length of the beach. Others were coming in and getting out behind them. Others were circling around picking up survivors from those that had been sunk.

Now that he knew we were on the beach Jerry was concentrating all he had on that stretch of sand. From each end there was the raking fire of machine-guns. From the cliffs and behind the town came heavy artillery shells which threw up huge showers of water as they landed in the sea among the boats. Mortar shells exploded on the beach and sent cascades of pebbles far and wide. Focke-Wulfs came running down low and spat their machine-gun and cannon fire at us. I watched a Junkers 88 that had managed to slip through our fighters come trundling (it seemed so slow and laborious compared to the speed of the Focke-Wulfs) along about a hundred feet above the beach and drops its bombs as it got over the boats.

The hazy smoke ... the little boats ... the men on the beach ... My mind flashed immediately to the newsreels and photographs I'd seen of Dunkirk. It was the same all over again on a smaller scale.

There didn't seem to be a square foot of that beach that something wasn't landing on. You looked down to the boats way off there at the water's edge and said to yourself that you'd never make it – the odds were too much against you.

I heard somebody shout to me, 'That's your boat there – along at the end!'

I dashed forward as fast as my legs would carry me, cursed as my army boots made me stumble on the loose pebbles. As I got on to the flat, wet sand I had the queer sensation of sailing through space the way you do in nightmares. My feet never seemed to touch the ground. The sound of explosions and the whistle of bullets rang in my ears, but I didn't think about the prospect of being hit or blown to bits. I thought about only one thing – getting to that boat.

Half-way down the beach I heard someone shout and turned my head to see what it was. A stretcher-bearer was standing there with a man on a stretcher lying at his feet. The other stretcher bearer had been killed, and he was trying to drag the wounded man alone down to the boats.

I pulled myself up and turned towards him. In times such as those your mind works at break-neck speed. 'Shall I go on or turn back to help these two men? Shall I save my own skin and to hell with them? No, it would be on my conscience for the rest of my life.'

But before I could get to them somebody else was there, and as I set off again for my boat I saw the stretcher being carried down to the water's edge.

I got a wonderful feeling of relief when I reached the boat. I'd thank my lucky stars. But the front ramp of the long steel landing craft wasn't down. It was up in the travelling position, which meant she was heading out to sea. I was preparing to clamber up over the side when I heard a voice say, 'She's stuck! We've got to push her off the sand!'

I waded into the water and joined the men who were now heaving and pushing at the sides of the craft. We'd get it out a few yards and feel that she was clear, only to have a wave buffet it back in again.

The water was salty and full of sand, and I found myself swallowing gritty, acrid mouthfuls of it. I kept as low down in the water as I possibly could, subconsciously thinking that that way I'd get some protection from the bullets that were flying about us.

I also figured quickly in my mind that as the enemy was up there behind the beach the safest spot would be on the far side of the landing craft, the side away from the beach. I worked my way round to that side and had only been there a second or two when a string of machine-gun bullets spattered along the steel side a few inches above my head.

I'd forgotten about those Focke-Wulfs! There was just *nowhere* on that beach where you could feel you were a little safer.

V

At last we got the craft out into deeper water. We could feel her gather momentum and head away from the beach. We grabbed hold of the rope dangling in long loops from the side of the craft and were dragged along through the water.

As we went I noticed the young lad next to me lose his grip. He grabbed frantically at the rope again, but the boat slipped away from him. He was too exhausted to swim after us, and I saw him standing waist-deep in the water, watching us go. I shall never forget the look on that boy's face. It was a look of utter hopelessness. He'd come so far, almost got onto the boat, and now we were going off without him.

That's how he felt at that moment. But he was soon to find out that dozens more boats were to make trips in to the beach to pick up men. He was probably taken off on one of those. I hope he did get back.

Hanging on by the ropes, we were packed shoulder to shoulder along each side of the landing craft, and it became more and more difficult to keep our grip in the swift current from the wash of the bow. My hands were cold and numb, and I had to loop an arm around the rope to stop myself from being cast adrift.

Some of the men had managed to clamber up the flat steel side of the craft on to the deck. Apart from the single rope hanging in loops from hooks about ten feet apart there was nothing to grab hold of to help yourself up. The steel was wet and slippery, and I hauled myself up by means of the rope, only to slither back again as I found nothing to grasp on the smooth, wet deck.

As I prepared to try again I heard a bullet whistle past my ear. It went right through the brains of the man next to me. He fell like a log, and his tin hat clanked against mine as he went down.

One minute he had been alive … and the next split second he was dead. It was as sudden as that.

He floated face downward on the water.

This time, as I got to the edge of the deck, a Navy lad got hold of my hands and started pulling me up. With the upper part of my body on the deck I seemed to get struck. He heaved as hard as he could, and I didn't have enough energy to make it easier for him.

Then someone down in the water locked himself round one of my leg and tried to pull himself up. As hard as the sailor would pull, as hard would the man below pull. I just lay there astride the boat and said to myself, 'Well boys, I'm in your hands – fight it out for yourselves.'

How eventually I did get up on to that deck I've no idea. But I do know that as soon as I was there I lay prone, my face against the cold steel plates, absolutely exhausted. I fought to get my breath back. I didn't care how exposed I was to enemy fire. I just wanted to rest.

Soon my spirits began to rise. I was on a boat headed away from Dieppe, headed towards England. Dieppe was all over now for me and the men down in the hold. It was jam-packed with men, many of them wounded. I'd go down there and join them in the comparative security of the hold in a minute, as soon as I could summon up enough energy to move.

Then a cry went up, 'We're sinking!'

I raised myself up and saw the bow end of the boat going down. Water started to pour into the hold, I saw it rising up higher and higher as the men down there got up onto their feet.

The water was up to their necks now, and it wasn't bluish-green water – it was red.

The little sailor who'd helped me on to the boat came running along the deck now. 'It's all right,' he said. 'Everything's okay. Just jump into the water and swim to that other boat over there.' He pointed to an empty landing craft that was circling us.

This Royal Navy lad was as cool as a cucumber. He didn't seem to be the least bit exercised about the situation. He gave us those instructions as calmly as if he'd been telling someone how to get from Oxford Circus to Piccadilly.

As I jumped into the water I took a glimpse back at the beach. To my amazement we weren't more than a couple of hundred yards off-shore. It seemed so long ago since we'd eventually got the craft off the sand and under way. But it hadn't been long. It had only been a few crowded, actionful minutes, and in that time the barge had been able to get only a short distance away from the beach before she was hit.

In the water I noticed something I hadn't realized before. There were dozens of tin hats floating on the surface.

Nearer to a landing craft further inshore there was a wounded soldier floating on the water in one of the buoyant stretchers they used for getting wounded out to ships. It looked to all intents and purposes like a venetian blind. It was strapped securely around him, and all I could see was his feet and head. He was lying on his back, his arms inside the stretcher. He was quite helpless. All he could do was lie there floating on the water while somebody pushed him out to a boat. Remembering the job we, with full use of our arms and legs, had had getting aboard a landing craft, I wondered how in God's name that they were going to get him aboard. How they did it, or if they did it, I don't know because at that moment the boat we'd been directed to came between me and the man I was watching. When I last saw him his head was right back, and he was looking up into the sky at the planes overhead – or perhaps he was looking further than that.

Now, all over again came the ordeal of climbing up the side of a landing craft. If nothing else we learned this lesson at Dieppe: our landing craft (so-called invasion barges) may be all right for disembarking and embarking troops on a beach in an orderly fashion, unmolested by the enemy, but when things go wrong and the men have to be taken aboard in deep water they're just about the most difficult boat to get into that one could imagine. When they are grounded ashore and the front ramp is lowered it's an easy matter to walk into them or drive a vehicle aboard, the way a car would be driven on to a river ferry. But once that front ramp is up (and it can't be lowered when the craft is at sea, because she'd immediately ship water and sink) the only way to get on board is to climb up the flat sides, which are four or five feet above the waterline.

The time wasted while men struggled to get into landing craft at Dieppe cost many lives – and unnecessarily. Most ships of the British Navy carry lengths of wide-mesh rope netting that is suspended out on a beam above the water when they're picking up men from the sea.

It would have been a simple matter to have had this type of rope netting suspended from each side of the landing craft, and it would have been no trick at all for the men to have climbed up it.

VI

It was thanks again to helping hands on deck that I managed to get up on to the second landing craft. But this time I didn't stay on deck. I went to the top of the hold and dived headfirst down into it.

I landed on the flat of my back on the steel bottom. It was a crazy thing to do, but I was past caring. From the top of the deck to the bottom of the hold was some seven feet. How I came out of that nose-dive without a bruise, let alone a broken bone, is beyond me.

I hadn't been there a second before other men came tumbling down on top of me. We became just a heap of fatigued bodies – arms and legs twisted round at all angles, saltwater oozing from your uniform, somebody's boot in the small of your back, a bandaged knee dripping blood pressed against your face.

I heard someone say, 'Get over to the side of the boat Make room!'

I pushed myself free and crawled over to the side, under the cover of the deck. More men dropped down into the hold from above. I became wedged in the mass of bodies. My arms were pinned by my sides. Someone was lying across my legs, and I couldn't move them. An injured soldier had collapsed across my chest and lay prone there so that I had to fight for breath.

I could hear bullets ricocheting off the deck above and hitting the outside of the boat. It was reassuring. You felt you were in shelter.

Then somebody shouted, 'Lighten ship! There are too many aboard! We're sinking!'

I saw a couple of men take their tin hats off and throw them up through the opening above into the sea. Water-bottles, webbing, bayonets, went flying out over the side.

'Take your boots off,' one of the men said, as he set to work trying to undo his sodden lacers.

'Take our clothes off! Everything! We've got lighten ship!'

Tunics came off, trousers, boots … As quickly as they could get them off they tossed them up over the side.

I struggled to get my arms free and then pulled the water-bottle from round my waist. I tossed my tin hat overboard and followed it with the water-bottle. As it went sailing through the air I caught a glimpse of the German helmet attached to it. Funny to think of at a time like that, but I remember having a twinge of regret as I saw it go. Too bad – it would have been a good souvenir to bring home.

A lot of the men had nothing left now but their underclothing. Clad only in their shorts, they went to work helping others to get their equipment and clothes off to throw them over the side.

I got to my feet and looked out on to the deck. Soldiers were still clambering up over the side. The more men who got on board the lower the boat sank down, until the deck now was almost flush with water.

I wasn't conscious of the ships around us. We seemed to be merely one craft and a lot of men in the midst of a hazy, grey smoke-screen.

There was a sailor moving among the men. He was a little guy. He was wearing a navy-blue sweater, blue slacks, and rubber shoes. He was skinny and frail-looking, as though he'd spent most of his life in the slums of London and needed a few good meals to fatten him up. He didn't need to open his mouth to let you know he was a Cockney. He had it written all over him.

He was moving along the deck, and he had a length of rope in his hand. What he was going to do with the rope I didn't know until a moment or two later.

Like the other Royal Navy lad – the one who had helped me into first landing craft – this boy was as calm and unflurried as if he was merely getting ready to throw the mooring-line up on to the wharf from a pleasure boat.

We were getting all worked up about the prospect of the craft sinking under us, of having to swim around in that water again and try to find some other boat to pick us up. But this kid – he was only in his teens – was giving us all a lesson in cool-headedness. He wasn't the least bit concerned about his own personal plight, the likelihood of gong down with the boat; he wasn't giving a single thought to the bullets flying about and the H.E exploding all around. He was the Navy at work. It was his job to save the boat and the men on it if he possibly could. He had work to do, and he wasn't to let any 'muck' that Jerry might fling at him make him less efficient.

I don't know why, but, watching that kid, seeing his courage and sheer guts, I wanted to cry. Maybe it was because I felt humble.

He was one end of the boat now, and I could see a ship coming towards us. It was an anti-aircraft ship, a small wooden vessel, and looked like a converted tug or a trawler. The Navy boy tossed his rope up on to the deck as she came alongside. We made fast to her and scrambled aboard.

VII

I picked my way through what seemed to be dozens of light-calibre anti-aircraft guns and plomped down on the deck with my back against the side of the bridge. I could feel the sun hot on my face, and steam started to rise out of my sodden uniform. But I was shivering and had to heave with my chest to get some wind.

But I felt pretty much at peace with the world. I'd come through it all, and now it was just a matter of relaxing there in the sun as we steamed back to England. It's moments like these that cigarettes are made for. I reached into a pocket of my tunic where I knew there was an unopened packet of Players. I thought the cellophane would have kept the water out, but I opened the packet only to find that its contents were a damp mess of soggy tobacco and brown-stained cigarette papers.

The man beside me had a specially waterproofed pack, and he handed them round. I noticed how thin and white my fingers were when I took the cigarette. They were numb, and it was an effort to hold on to it properly. But I never did get that cigarette smoked. I passed it on to somebody else and said, 'Here, you take this. I'll have one later.' I didn't have enough breath left to smoke it.

The ship got under way, and I stretched out and closed my eyes.

But in a moment or two I heard the men around me getting to their feet. I opened my eyes and saw we were coming alongside a destroyer.

'Climb aboard,' somebody said.

'And another voice, 'What, again? Good God!'

Chapter 11

On the Headquarters Destroyer

I

We were helped up on to the destroyer. Its decks were already thick with troops. I walked through a doorway leading to a covered part of the main deck. I didn't know quite where I was going, but the men who had got aboard before me were going that way, so I followed them.

I felt a tap on my shoulder, and an officer said, 'Go down this companion-way, War Correspondent. The ward-room's there. You'll find some pals there – Quentin Reynolds for one.'

I slithered down the metal ladder and felt my feet plop onto the floor. My boots were still full of water. Funny how your thoughts run … I remember recalling to mind that I'd bought these boots the day before I started on this trip. The salesman had told me that 'these boots are guaranteed to be watertight.' I said to myself I'd return to the store as soon as possible as I got back in London and tell the salesman I'd found the boots watertight all right – I'd got them full of water and not a drop had leaked out.

I staggered into the ward-room and fell flat on my face on the floor.

A red-headed steward brought some brandy, and a couple of slugs of it made me feel considerably better. My wet uniform was taken off, and clad merely in my shorts with a blanket wrapped around me, I sunk into one of those large black leather armchairs. I sipped the remains of the liberal tumbler of Three-Star Hennessy the steward had poured me and took a look round the room.

The destroyer was small – a Hunt class, smallest type of British destroyer and only about nine hundred tons. The reason I knew it was a Hunt was that I noticed a fox's tail mounted on a wooden shield hanging above the electric fireplace.

The ward-room ran the entire width of the ship – some thirty feet – and was ten or twelve feet wide. One half of the room was occupied by the Mess table, with the bar-opening in the wall beside it. The other half contained a fireplace, a long couch against the side of the ship, two big armchairs, in one of which I was sitting, and a glass-fronted cupboard full of books.

There were about fifteen men in the room when I got there. Two injured Navy officers were stretched out under blankets on the couch, other wounded were lying asleep on the floor, and there were several men seated at the Mess table, one or two of them lying with their faces down on their arms on the table trying to get some rest.

I noticed the clock on the far end of the wall said ten minutes past twelve. It had taken us exactly one hour and three boats to get out the mile or so off the beach to this destroyer.

The brandy was beginning to bring on a warm glow, and I began to feel quite pepped up. I did some mental arithmetic.

'A destroyer of this type,' I said to myself, 'can do anything up to thirty knots. Supposing it's about sixty miles back to England. We'll high-tail it out of here and be back in a couple of hours – two and a half hours at the outside. Brother! Things are looking up!'

But I was in for a rude awakening. As things developed we didn't leave Dieppe until after three o'clock that afternoon. For three solid hours we were to circle close to the shore to pick up survivors.

I was scared skinny every minute of it.

We had time, loads of time to be scared. It was not like being out in the open there, with something to do, something to occupy your mind. We had nothing to do but just sit there while the shore batteries tried to land artillery shells on us, dive-bombers roared down on us, and enemy fighter planes swooped low and peppered our ship with their machine-guns and cannon.

We were hemmed in there in that small space down in the bowels of the ship. We knew that if we did sink we'd have just no chance – the decks and the companion-ways above us were so crowded with men that we wouldn't have a hope of getting up and out as she went down.

For those of us down below there was acute claustrophobia, plus the knowledge that if the ship were sunk we'd go down with her. The hundreds of men up on the open decks were free of this hemmed-up, trapped-like-rats feeling, but for them there was the hell of seeing Focke-Wulfs coming down at them, seeing their pilots open up their guns as they reached the stern and go the whole length of the ship a mere few feet overhead, raking the vessel from stern to bow, spitting their machine-guns bullets and cannon shells into the mass of men crowded on the decks.

II

Corporal Joe Gregory was one of the men up there. Joe's forty-two, and a veteran of the last war. Talking to me when we got back, he told me that for concentrated hell-fire he'd never experienced anything like Dieppe in the 1914–18 business.

Joe was shot in the eye as he was coming off the beach. He managed to get out to a motor gunboat. His eye was examined, he was told he would never have the sight of it again, he was bandaged up and put in the sick-bay. He was no sooner there than the ship was dive-bombed. A huge hole was blown in the side of the sick-bay. The water poured in, and Joe thought his end had come. But the backwash washed him right out of the hole, and he was picked up and brought to our destroyer.

Every sick-bay on the ship was crowded – over-crowded – so like dozens of us other wounded Joe had to settle himself down somewhere. He lay down on the deck beside an Oerlikon anti-aircaft gun. 'The noise,' he says, 'was something terrible. But I was beyond caring about a mere thing like noise. I just passed out there and then.'

He didn't wake up until several hours later. He looked out across the water, and there he could see the white cliffs. He turned to the gunner and asked: 'Holy Jesus, we're pretty near home!' The gunner said, 'Home be buggered – we're still at Dieppe!'

As the Germans turned on everything they could to try and blow the flotilla of ships out of the sea, Joe and the others up on deck could watch it all, get a vivid picture of what was happening. We down below

were like an audience at a talkie that had broken down – the screen
blank and the sound track still going on. We could hear the explosives
and the anti-aircraft, but what was happening we had to visualize in
our minds.

There is nothing that's quite as calculated to tear at your nerves as
that. We had to experience the whole thing through one of our five
senses - our hearing. It was all a series of different sounds, each with
its own meaning, each fitting into a pattern that we came to know
by heart.

The fire-control mechanism (by which the fire of the anti-aircraft
gun is directed) had been put out of action. So, to get the ship into
position so that a maximum of ack-ack fire could be directed at an
approaching dive-bomber, the engine-room telegraph was used. The
engineers would be told to increase speed on the port or starboard
propeller, as the case might be, so that the ship could slew round into
a better position.

One of the controls of this engine-room telegraph was in a box
just above our heads in the ceiling of the ward-room. Whenever the
telegraph was used this box would give out a sequence of *rat-a-tats*.

When we heard this racket we knew that one or two things was
going to happen. Either we were about to be dive-bombed ... or we
were going home to England!

The ship's engines were idling as we circled about off-shore. They
made a barely perceptible drone. They'd have to be revved up when we
started for home, and the way to speed them up was for instructions to
come from the bridge to the telegraph.

So there it would come, that clanging *rat-a-tat*, and we'd sit and
wonder – does it mean the engines are being revved and we're off
home, or are we going to be dive-bombed? We'd strain our ears to
catch the first sounds of what we hoped would be a deepening throb
of the engines, the ship vibrating as extra steam was put on – and off
we'd go! Instead we'd hear a slight quickening of speed on one of the
propellers. We were going to be dive-bombed. We'd wait for the next
sound, the one we'd know would automatically follow.

Our 4.7 ack-ack gun would open up. That was the heaviest calibre gun, the first one to take a crack at the approaching plane, while it was way off there in the distance. Then as it came into dive the single pom-pom would start. *Pom... pom... pom... pom...* A dull monotonously regular pounding. Then the rowdy clattering of the Oerlikon gun. The bomber's getting close now. The Lewis guns break into a rattle as it's practically on top of us.

You steel yourself, tense every muscle in your body, and wait for the explosion.

A miss, thank God. You hear the bomb explode in the water in the distance.

Then all the ship's ack-ack guns sound off again. This time in reverse, starting up with the small clattering guns and working up to the boom of the 4.7 – they're firing at the bomber as she goes away.

We knew that these bombers were diving at us broadside on, because our guns would start pounding away on the port side, say, and then they'd stop, and the guns would take over the target on the starboard.

Each time we were dive-bombed I'd involuntarily turn my back to the side the attack was coming from, switch to the other side as the plane went across us. I've no idea what good I thought this manoeuvre was doing me, for had a bomb landed in the water outside that thin steel plating that divided us in the ward-room from the sea the mere fact of having my back to the explosion wouldn't have delayed in the slightest my take-off to smithereens. It was just one of those things you do without giving it any thought, like automatically recoiling when a baseball comes flying at the wire-netting in front of you.

The plating of a destroyer's hull is only about three-sixteenths of an inch thick. Compared to the several-inches thickness of a battleship's, or that of other larger naval vessels, a destroyer's hull is flimsy, to say the least. Reason for this is that thickness of plating and weight of plating have been sacrificed to get speed. Destroyers can do twenty-six to thirty knots – some of them well over thirty. They can even do twenty knots in reverse – which is something I'd like to witness some day. In two-reel comedies we've often seen the film run through backward and people diving out of a swimming-pool back up on to the spring-board, cars scurrying along the streets backwards. A destroyer batting along at twenty knots stern first would be my idea of turning the tables on the movie-camera pranksters.

If you want to realize fully just how flimsy a destroyer's sides are you need do nothing more than tap them with your knuckles and hear the ominously tinny rattle. Once a destroyer was moored in harbour, and a speedboat was breezing around. It got out of control and hit the destroyer. It went clean through the hull and finished up on the floor of the ward-room.

Chapter 12

In the Ward-room

I

I started chatting with the two naval officers who were lying on the couch beside my chair. They were both naked, save for the blankets wrapped around them. Not many of us in the ward-room had any clothes on – our uniforms were either hanging up on the wall with the salt water dripping from them, or they'd been taken down to the boiler-room to dry out there.

These two men were both badly injured. The special service craft they'd been on had had a direct hit on the magazine and had blown up. Only a handful of men had survived, and they'd floated about on a raft during these early stages of the battle when ships and landing craft were moving in to the beaches to be greeted by blasting fire from the shore batteries.

'We owe our lives to our ship's M.O. [medical officer],' one of them said. 'There were half a dozen or so of us on the raft. We were all badly knocked about. It's a terrible feeling lying there in agony like that, with all hell popping around you. Some of the men wanted to jump into the water and just swim off – anywhere. But we stopped them. When you're hurt and you've got nothing to do but just lie where you are you get an awful hopeless, helpless feeling.

'But then the M.O. came swimming up to us. He climbed on to the raft, and you've no idea what a difference he made to our spirits. We were bucked up right away. He examined each of us and told us what was wrong. There wasn't much he could do about anything; he didn't have the equipment. But I dunno … you seemed to get the reassuring feeling that you were under medical care, that you were being looked after.

'He's wonderful that M.O. His name's Martin. He's on the ship now, practically dropping from fatigue. He and this ship's M.O. are the only doctors on board, apart from the sick-bay attendants, and there are hundreds of wounded and dying on board, as you know. He hasn't rested a second. He just keeps going back and forth along the decks, up and down the companion-ways, in and out of the sick-bays, looking after the men. He's coming back to look at us, to see how we are getting along. He'll be here soon, and you'll meet him.'

Martin arrived in the ward-room in a few minutes. He was dressed in a sports jacket, grey flannels and white tennis shoes he'd borrowed from another officer on board. He was small-built, young, good-looking. He sank down on to the bench that stood round the front of the fireplace and talked to the two men on the couch. He was soft-spoken, and there was a warmth about him. A good guy – you could tell in a second.

You didn't need to be told he was tired. He was utterly worn out; his head swayed from side to side as he spoke.

Somebody said to him, 'You should rest up a minute or two. Here, let's get you a drink.'

Martin nodded. 'Yes, I think that would be a good idea.'

But he didn't pause long over his drink. He soon went back to looking over the condition of the men in the ward-room. When he came to me I said I didn't feel like letting him waste his time looking at the nick I had in my bottom.

'Let's have a look at it.'

He decided it might be merely a nick made by a shell-splinter in passing or the fragment might have gone right in. He advised me to get an X-ray when I got back.

As I had to go to work immediately after Dieppe writing my story, it wasn't until several weeks later, when I was in Canada, that I had the chance to have an X–ray. It revealed a shell-splinter deep in, near to the bone.

I joined the throng of men who were in the last war, this war, and countless other wars who have been shot in the bottom. We're different, quite apart from other war casualties, for, more than any other sort of injury, ours is one with a very strong comedy angle. It's well-nigh impossible to get any sympathy for a punctured posterior. Your friends trot out all the limitless variations of 'It certainly shows which way you were running.' (Laughter.) The whole thing's a joke in which you invariably join, despite the fact that you had to lie on your face for a week or so after the operation for the removal of the shrapnel, and then when you were up and about again you would sit down on a chair only after making a couple of light-pressure landings on it.

My wife always taxes me with the fact that I take a poor photograph, asks me when I'm going to have a good one taken for her to keep. She was in hospital when I was X-rayed, and even she couldn't resist the temptation when the X-ray was shown to us of saying, 'Darling, it's the best likeness you've ever had.'

In joining the ranks of those who had been hit below the belt I've also come to experience the phenomenon of having one's wound react to the state of the weather, felt the twinges of pain down there foretell the coming of rain. Though I'm never likely to be caught out of doors in a cloudburst without a raincoat, I regard it as a dubious privilege to have a barometric bottom.

II

As Martin was about to leave, one of the naval officers on the couch called to him, 'I say, doc. Do you think you could send down a jug or something? I can't get up and –'

'Oh sure. I'll have it sent in.'

A sick-bay attendant brought the white enamel jug, and the man accepted it with thanks.

But a moment or two later I happened to look over in his direction, and there was a pained expression on his face.

'I don't know what's wrong,' he said. 'I've waited a long time for this. I've looked forward to it. And what happens? Nothing? You fellows must be making me bashful or something.'

He abandoned the project for the time being. But others of us embraced this welcome opportunity to perform what in times of stress always seemed to be an increasingly recurrent function, and soon we were handing around what we came to call the loving-cup.

III

The time dragged on. It got to be one o'clock, and still there was no sign of us heading home.

The senior engineer dropped in from time to time. A tall, powerfully built Scot, he was wearing what looked like earmuffs over his ears. Actually they're padded protection for the eardrums, to guard against their being shattered by the blast of an explosion.

Every time the engineer officer appeared at the doorway we flooded him with questions? 'When are we going to leave?' we'd ask him. And every time would come back the grinning reply, 'Any time now.'

Talking to Quentin Reynolds, I learned our ship was H.M.S. *Calpe*, the headquarters ship of the operation, and Major-General Roberts, who had charge of the military forces, was in his cabin up above supervising getting his men off the beaches.

'I've just been up on the bridge,' Reynolds said, 'Believe it or not, we've moved closer to the beach. After talking to General Roberts my guess is that we're going to be the last to leave the scene. He's not going to leave until he's darn sure every man who can be gotten off *has* been gotten off.'

We decided to have something to eat. The last meal I'd had was twelve hours ago, and that was a supper at about one o'clock in the morning on the transport ship crossing the Channel.

Somebody had a box of twenty-four-hour rations, and opened it up. We helped ourselves to biscuits and opened a tin of sardines and some canned meat.

The sardine on my biscuit looked very appetizing as I raised it to my mouth, but before I could bite into it there was an interruption. There was a terrific explosion, the ship jolted, and my biscuit and sardine shot across the room. It must have been a shell from one of the shore batteries, because it was so unexpected, and there hadn't been the familiar warning of ack-ack fire that always preceded a bomb attack.

The crash came right at the side of the ship, and in a moment water started pouring in through the door of the ward-room.

I said to myself, 'This is it. This is the end.'

I jumped up as the other men did and headed for the door. There wouldn't be much chance of getting up and out of the ship, but you could at least go down trying.

But at the doorway we were greeted by the cheery grin of the red-headed steward.

'There's nothing to worry about,' he said. 'It's only a shell-splinter that's punctured the sprinkler system, All it will do is put out your cigarettes.'

This steward – he was about twenty, and his face was as ruddy as his hair – was among other things self-appointed chief of the morale department of the ward-room. As we settled down again he produced from somewhere two plates heaped high with meat sandwiches. He was at great pains to see nobody lacked a drink.

When he brought the brandy bottle round to refill our glasses I reached for the soggy role of notes that had been in my battle-dress, which I was now drying out on the mantelpiece.

As I peeled off a note he shook his head and said, 'I don't think the Navy will expect you to pay for this one, chum.'

Late in the afternoon, 'Red' disappeared for half an hour or so. Nobody could find him anywhere. He eventually turned up again as bright as ever and confessed to us he'd been 'sleeping it off.' His generosity with the brandy bottle he had extended to himself also while going the rounds, and he'd suddenly found himself plastered and passed out.

IV

As we sat eating our sandwiches a naval officer appeared at the door. He was young, boyish-looking, tall and slim. His face was covered with blood , which was streaming down from a gash at the top of his head. His shirt wasn't white any more, it was red.

We helped him into one of the easy-chairs, and the blood was cleaned away from the wound.

'It was a splinter from that shell,' he said.

Martin came in and looked at it.

'Don't bother with me,' said the officer. 'It's nothing. There are others up there who are much worse off.'

The M.O. put a dressing on the wound, and the officer insisted again that he should go up to the other injured. Martin said, 'Okay,' and told him he'd be back later to have another look at him.

I handed the officer – his name was Beale – my glass of brandy, but he shook his head.

'No, thanks. I don't drink. But I would like a glass of water.'

I brought him some, but when I offered him a cigarette he said he didn't smoke.

'I just want to sit here quietly for a while,' he said.

He closed his eyes and leaned his head gently back on to the top of the chair. He bit his lower lip, and his fingers, stretched out one round the arm of the chair, dug into the black leather padding. He was obviously going through hell.

I asked him again, but he assured me he didn't want anything; all he wanted to do was rest there, so I didn't bother him any further.

I looked over towards him now and again and then as the time crept slowly by, he remained in that same position. His face was deathly white, and a trickle of blood had worked its way across his neck. There were times when he seemed on the point of collapsing. But he held on tight and just shook his head when others went up to him and asked whether they could do anything.

He didn't move out of that chair once during all the hours we were off-shore from the beaches and crossing the Channel. Not until we were getting towards the home port did he stir.

I felt moved by the display of guts of this young officer. I suppose Beale was what a lot of people who don't understand the English or care to go about trying to understand them would term 'a stuffy Englishman'. Stiff, stand-offish, no fun at all, Doesn't smoke, doesn't drink. Some may have thought it a joke when a little later he asked for another glass of water. By that time there was an acute shortage of glasses. I couldn't find one, so I poured some water into an empty brandy bottle and handed it to him. He was hesitant about taking it, and asked, 'This is water, isn't it?' When I assured him it was he drank, and then when he was through, looked up at me and said: 'That was strong. That had brandy in it.'

But for reasons of his own Beale had decided against touching liquor, and he wasn't going to let the confusion of battle and stress of battle deflect him from the path he'd chosen on that score. He was as sincere and earnest about that as he was about not letting the Royal Navy down. He'd been injured, and he knew he wasn't any use any more up on deck. But he also knew that there were more injured men on board than the two overworked M.O.s and the sick-bay attendants could cope with. He'd stick it there in his chair and hold out until we got home. He didn't want to take up an M.O.'s time that he felt could be much better spent on somebody else.

I know why he didn't want to let the Navy down. It was because he felt the same way about the British Navy that everybody who has seen it in action feels – it is something quite on another plane from anything else, from any other endeavour that man has turned his hand to.

I've had long chats with fellow-newspapermen and other people who've been on destroyers and other ships of the Navy. I mean outsiders, non-Navy men, who have by good fortune had the opportunity to watch the men of the Navy at work at close quarters. We talked it over, discussed it from every angle, and tried to define what makes the British Navy.

The closest I can come to putting it into words is to say it's a thousand and one little things. It's that young officer there in the ward-room sticking it out. It's the chirpy red-headed steward who never wasted a moment's thought on the destroyer sinking with him in it. It's little Cockneys bringing loads of troops off the beaches in landing craft and then turning their boats around again and heading back into the hell of those beaches to get more men ... Never does it enter their heads – any of them, whether they have gold braid on their sleeves or merely wear dungarees, it just doesn't occur to them – to think about their own skin. There's a job to be done, and if they get killed doing it, well, that's just one of those things.

Perhaps the best way to define the British Navy is not to attempt to describe it, but instead to point out something that is unique.

I have never heard anybody say anything against the British Navy. Now, no matter in how high repute a personage, organization, or anything may be held by the public, there is always some who will say, 'But Churchill is bad when it comes to this ...' or, 'The Rockies are beautiful, but ...' Yet in the British Navy you have something that even the most ardent haters of the British and things British, whether they are isolationists or members of the Axis, cannot bring themselves to denounce.

The British Navy is a thing apart.

V

It ticked by to after two o'clock. I'd been in that ward-room for two hours now. The engineer officer came up from below again, and we asked him when he was going to put those engines into top gear and start us off home.

'Any time now ...'

He was as much in the dark about our time of departure as we were.

The two injured Navy men on the couch got into a discussion as to how fast the destroyer would carry us home. One said a Hunt class could do thirty knots full out; the other said twenty-seven. We got down to *Jane's Fighting Ships*, that bible of the Navy which lists every fighting ship in the world and its performance, and settled the argument. We'd be going home at twenty-seven knots ...

The room was getting more crowded now. An American Ranger named Schwank was brought in badly hurt, and one of the men on the couch gave up his place for him. Schwank lay face downward and slept.

He was one of several American troops I encountered at Dieppe. There had been another Ranger on the transport ship going over. His name was Bob Flanagan, a lieutenant from Houston, Texas. I'd asked Flanagan what part he was taking in the raid, and he explained to me that the small detachment of Rangers was going over chiefly as observers. The Rangers are the American equivalent of the British Commandos, and Flanagan and the others were going into the fighting with raiding troops, to pick up all the pointers they could about how these things are done, and then when they got back, make out reports that would be helpful in the training of their own men. They were armed, and naturally if they got the chance to get to grips with the enemy they would. They were spread out in small groups and attached to various regiments, in the same way that we war correspondents were.

It was unfortunate that a misunderstanding arose as to the extent of the American participation in the raid. I know when we got back it riled the Canadian troops to read in the London papers a reprint of the headlines which had appeared in some sections of the American press, 'U.S. and British invade France'.

In point of fact, there were fewer than fifty Americans taking part. The Rangers themselves and the Headquarters Staff of the U.S. Army in Britain felt as badly about it as did the Canadians, who'd made up five-sixths of the land forces engaged. To a Press conference in London at Combined Operations Headquarters immediately after the raid the U.S. Forces sent a General, no less, with the express purpose of urging American correspondents to play down American participation in the raid. As they were just back from the raid and hadn't as yet written anything on it, the correspondents were only too willing to cooperate, and in fact sent a service message to every newspaper editor in the States, explaining just how small had been the U.S. detachment.

The American newspapers were not entirely to blame. The root of the trouble lay in the poor handling of the raid by Combined Operations as far as Press releases were concerned. In the early stages when the first news started filtering through it was not made clear just who had been participating and to what extent.

VI

In the ward-room it soon became no longer possible to walk across the room – it was a matter of picking your way across the floor carefully over the recumbent bodies, making sure as you put your foot down that you didn't tread on some one's injured leg or bump your head against a bandaged back.

Most of the men were Canadian army officers. No one had much to say. Most were asleep. Others just sat there in their chairs and listened to the engine telegraph rattling, and the ack-ack guns, and the leisurely, almost inaudible throb of the engines as they kept the ship barely moving up and down in front of the beach …

Quentin Reynolds, alone of anybody at this time, was reading. He devoured two or three detective novels from the ship's library in no time and will admit to you now that he can't remember the plot of a single one of them.

One of the men was delirious. Ashore, as he'd taken his platoon well inland he'd been shot in the side, in the thigh, and the leg. He hadn't been able to climb into the landing craft coming out, and dangling from the rope on the side of the boat he'd found himself being towed out to the destroyer. He talked now about the pals he'd known for years who had been killed before his eyes.

VII

Another destroyer near us, H.M.S. *Berkeley*, was hit and had to be sunk by our own forces. We were picking up her survivors now, and some of them were brought into the ward-room.

One was Fred Clarke, a Canadian Air Force lad from Calgary. His right eye was bandaged. He'd been flying a Mustang and back behind the town he'd run into a Focke-Wulf 190. In the fight his engine was hit but luckily not put out of action. The prop. still chugged over, even if sporadically. He found his plane losing height. He couldn't see very clearly, because something had hit him the eye. The pain was excruciating, his vision blurred, but he turned the plane towards the Channel.

He was about six miles inland, and the plane was slowing up so much by then it was more like being at the controls of a glider than a fighter.

He steered over the beach and realized then that'd he'd never make England. So he decided to land on the water. He put her down smoothly on the water, right alongside a destroyer. He was taken on board. I noticed the uniform he was wearing as perfectly dry – he must have made a perfect landing all right.

Dieppe was the first operational flight Fred Clarke had ever been on.

Chapter 13

Back to England

I

A little over three o'clock the engineer officer appeared at the doorway. His took his ear pads off and said, 'Well boys, any time now we'll be headed home.'

We didn't show much enthusiasm. We'd heard that before. As the time dragged on we'd asked everybody who'd come into the wardroom from up above whether we were moving, whether we showed any signs of moving out to sea. Each of them had said, 'Sure, we're moving,' and then, on pressure for more information, had qualified it by saying that we were going around in circles. But always added was the remark, 'We'll be leaving soon, there's no doubt about that.' Among other things, the men of the Royal Navy are past masters at looking on the bright side.

The engineer officer burst into a grin when he saw our casual reaction to his news were about to go.

'It's a fact this time,' he said.

And sure enough, in a moment or two the engines started to increase speed.

You felt inside you, Thank God – at last.

We heard the crash of heavier guns up above.

'That's our farewell to Dieppe,' said the officer.

'We've been hit a couple of times,' he added, 'and we're shipping a bit of water here and there. But we'll get you home all right.'

He replaced his ear pads and went below.

I made a note of the time by the clock on the wall. Ten past three. It was exactly ten hours and twenty minutes since I'd arrived at Dieppe with the first landing craft to touch down on the beaches.

Our destroyer was the last to leave the scene, so that meant I had the doubtful privilege of being among those who had been first in and last out at Dieppe.

As we got under way the engines didn't seem to be giving the hearty throb that I'd learned to associate with destroyers at speed. I remembered the first trip I did in a destroyer, on a convoy patrol on the North Atlantic. I'd been impressed at the way the engines could be made to respond with a roar to the call for speed. That ship hadn't merely got under way – she'd taken off. But no such burst of speed came from the engines of this ship. We wondered what was holding us back.

Then we learned something that completely scrubbed out the picture we'd built up in our minds of our ship breezing back across the Channel like a bat out of hell.

Somebody came into the ward-room. He'd just been on the bridge. He told us that we were not going back at full speed. We had to escort slower craft, so we were going at much reduced speed.

This was yet another contribution to the long series of having our spirits go up, only to have them dashed again. The relief of getting across that beach to the landing craft alive, to find that the boat had to be pushed off the sand – climbing aboard, thinking we'd go home right away on that boat, then having it sink under us – reaching the destroyer, feeling all our troubles were over now and we'd speed back over the Channel, only to have to wait for hours a little way off the beaches. Now we had a long, slow crossing to look forward to, a trundling target for the bombers, more dive-bombing, more enemy fighters swopping down at us. When would it ever end?

II

I got to thinking I would never come out of it alive.

But I had to. I must. After everything I'd seen and been through, I had to write the story. I had to get back to England alive, get a typewriter and get it all on paper. It would just have been my bad luck to come this far, to have the material for the biggest story I'd ever had in my life, one of the biggest single stories of the war … and then to be blotted out on the way home.

The thought kept racing through my mind, I shan't make it – I shan't get back – and that will be the end of my life untidily – it's not rounded off neatly – there's unfinished business – I've got all the material gathered but nothing on paper yet …

And then I thought about all the other men, the ones who had been killed – the soldier who'd been getting into the landing craft beside me and a bullet had gone through his brain and he'd floated away face downward in the water. He had unfinished business too; maybe he had a youngster back in Canada who'd been born after he'd left for overseas and he'd never seen. Perhaps as he was about to die he thought, 'If only I could have seen my son just once I'd die happy. To die now is leaving loose ends in my life …'

I wonder why our minds run like that. Faced with the prospect of death, you think about all the things you were on the verge of getting done, the things that would be left undone when you're killed right then.

I thought about the trip I'd planned to take back to Canada. I was on the point of going when Dieppe turned up. I'd have seen my wife again. If only I could set eyes on her again I wouldn't mind dying.

Or at least I thought I shouldn't mind dying.

I have seen her again. As I write this she is seated here in the same room with me. But I still don't want to die. I'm not ready to die. When the time comes again and I'm close up beside death there'll be other things I'll say I must get done before I die. There'll be other unfinished business …

Right at this second I don't want to die because this book isn't finished. When this book is finished, okay, I'll be ready to die …

That's what I kid myself.

III

As I sat in the ward-room on the edge of the seat that ran round the front of the fireplace I happened to overhear the word 'submarine'.

Off went my mind on another tangent. Torpedoes. I hadn't thought about that angle. My mind added the submarine menace to the list of ways the destroyer might be sunk. At that moment perhaps a German submarine had us in the sight of his periscope.

I yearned for something to do. Getting ashore there at dawn ... moving about in the streets ... getting off the beach ... I hadn't any of this churning around inside me at the prospect of being killed. I was out and about ... had lots of things to do ... no time to sit and just left my mind go off on tangents.

I went over to the ship's library and picked up a book and returned to my seat. I could at least read.

It was by that well-known writer of sea stories, ' Taffrail'. Its title: *Dover-Ostend: A Cross-Channel Thriller.*

I had a good laugh over that one.

I looked around the men in the ward-room. I envied those who could sleep through it. I looked at the others sitting up in their chairs and wondered how they felt about it all. And I came to see what training means. Drilling, marching, spit and polish, P.T.... all those things that the newly joined-up soldier dislikes so much and about which he'll ask, 'What the hell's the point of all this?' Well. this was the point of it. Those men I the ward-room with me were trained soldiers equipped mentally and physically to stand up to this sort of thing.

IV

The engines started increasing speed. We were going faster now. The heavier throb was comforting and reassuring.

For a time it was.

Then we learned the reason for it.

The red-headed steward poked his head through the doorway.

'I thought I might mention,' he said 'that we're just entering a minefield.'

Someone asked, 'Why have we just increased speed?'

'That's General Roberts' orders. He wanted the headquarters ship to be the first of the flotilla to go through.'

'That means if any ship's going to hit a mine this'll be the one to do it.'

'That's right.'

'Thanks for the cheery information.'

'Oh, we'll get through all right.'

And we did get through all right. That in itself is a tribute to the Navy. Of the several hundred ships and boats that went to and returned from Dieppe, not a single one was lost hitting a mine. How the Navy was able to shepherd that vast flotilla of vessels through those mine-studded enemy coastal waters without a casualty is something that leaves the layman lost for words.

We were well out into the Channel now. The time crept on to seven o'clock ... eight o'clock ... It must be starting to get dark now.

Our friend the engineer officer appeared in the doorway, to be greeted by the query 'When are we getting into port?'

'About midnight.'

'Midnight! Holy mackerel!'

V

It was about half past twelve when we came alongside the wharf. A short time before we reached port one of the sick-bay attendants had come round and taken particulars of our injuries.

He had with him a sheet of paper ruled off in three columns headed 'Cot Cases', 'Walking Injured' and 'Uninjured'. As he checked with each of us he put a stroke in the appropriate column.

I took my uniform from the hook on the wall but it seemed to be still wet and sodden as when I came out of the water, so I decided against putting it on. Few of us had dry clothes, so it was just a matter of going ashore in our underwear with blankets wrapped round us. But rather than go barefoot I put on my wet boots. Quentin Reynolds presented me with a pair of dry socks, which he had in his haversack. It was a pair he had bought in Moscow while covering the Russian front a few months previously.

With my uniform bundled under my arm and a blanket around my shoulders, I filed up the companion-way with the other men. It was pitch black on deck but as we walked down the gangway to the dock there seemed to be plenty of light. The authorities had struck a compromise between strictly observing the blackout and having sufficient light to disembark the hundreds of men with a minimum of delay and soldiers moved about with hurricane lamps. Their glaring beams of light lit up the shapes of ambulances, trucks and mobile canteens lined along the dock. There were lots of Canadian troops there to welcome their companions back from the raid, help them into ambulances, serve hot tea and refreshments to those who didn't have to go to hospital.

The first soldier I met as I stepped off the gangway placed a packet of Canadian cigarettes in my hand. It was a gift from a Toronto organization. Not a single man stepped off that destroyer without having cigarettes given to him.

Though glad to be back on solid ground again, I felt tired and worn out as I climbed into an Army Press car with Reynolds and Lieutenant Lockyear, an official Army photographer who had also been on the raid, and set off for a hotel. Rather than go straight up to London, we'd decided to stay the night and go there in the morning.

The streets were dark and bleakly deserted as we drove along. We were back in the depressing gloom of the blackout, and I was beginning to feel a reaction set in. I'd known it would come sooner or later. One can't keep up a high pitch of excitement and ward off indefinitely the reaction to a quick succession of shocks and ordeals. I felt myself wanting to be driven on and on in that car as far away from the scene as possible … to get completely away from it all. I resolved right there and then that I'd catch the next Clipper across the Atlantic, find myself a cottage in the backwoods, somewhere where life was quiet and peaceful, and live out the rest of my days there.

At Dieppe I'd seen action, been under enemy fire for the first time in my life. It was something I had yearned for in the months I had been covering the war. Well, I'd been under fire … and it was hell. I was going to get as far away from it as I possibly could.

That was my immediate reaction. But as I write this Dieppe is several months past and I realize that my first excursion into the firing line is akin to a woman having a baby. In the throes of it all she vows that the agony is something well nigh impossible for human nature to stand. Never again will she submit herself to it. But she does. Now I await eagerly - in fact I'm impatient for – the day of having my second baby.

VI

As we walked into the hotel hobby I noticed several groups of people in the lounge having drinks. I adjusted my blanket to make sure I wasn't making too revealing an entrance. But I needn't have taken the trouble. Nobody was the least bit concerned about the state of our attire. The night porter signed us in as casually as if he'd been receiving any everyday guests and I realized that this particular port has long since become accustomed to the sight of people arriving semi-clad and dishevelled from misadventures on the high seas.

So blasé was the porter about the whole thing that as he took up in the elevator to our room he didn't feel it necessary to inquire how we'd arrived in our sorry state. What was more vivid in his mind was the air raid the town had had that day. He conveyed the news of the raid to us and, after a long disquisition on the affair, concluded by remarking, 'I've had a helluva day.' We turned on him and in unison came back with 'You've had a helluva day!'

We sank into the fresh, clean sheets of our beds and were asleep as our heads touched the pillows. But I awoke with a start about half an hour later. We were still in the ship. We were about to be dive-bombed. I was convinced of it. There it was again, the regular *pom ... pom ... pom ...* of the single pom-pom anti-aircraft gun.

It was a few seconds before I gathered what the noise really was. A staircase was right beside one of the walls of our room and some of the people I'd seen down in the lounge were now making their way leisurely way up to bed, their footsteps beating an out an altogether too familiar rhythm on the carpeted stairway.

For days afterwards any everyday sound that was the least bit like one of those that had been assailing our ears the whole time we were on the streets and on the beaches of Dieppe sent my mind flashing back.

I resumed my sleep but was awakened again at seven o'clock in the morning. What woke me this time was the town's air raid sirens. They were followed closely by the sound of planes overhead.

An air raid. My God, I thought to myself, when was this thing ever going to end? There seemed to be no let-up, no end to it all. It seemed to go on and on and on. Here we lay in a bed in England but Dieppe wasn't finished yet.

And it struck me that right there was the key to the most effective way of attacking a person's morale. My morale at that point was something close in the vicinity of zero. And the reason for it was that I was worn out, exhausted. I'd been through experiences that were new and strange to me, which were shattering to my nerves. I was ready to go off for a while somewhere and regain my physical and mental balance. But bang on top of it all came an air raid.

It gave me an insight into an opinion I'd often heard expressed and taken for granted without having given much thought to it. 'Round the clock bombing is the only way that it's possible to really undermine civilian morale. It can't be done by sporadic raids however heavy they are.' As a non-combatant in a coastal battle, untrained and without any previous experience of being under enemy fire, I had been in exactly the same situation as a civilian in a severe air raid. I was taking no part in the proceedings, had no means at my disposal of retaliating or of checking the onslaught to which I was exposed.

But once the battle was over I had a feeling of untold relief – I felt the way everyone feels when the All Clear goes. Thank goodness that's over.

But it wasn't over. Getting on board the destroyer hadn't been the end of the raid, setting off for England wasn't saying goodbye to the dive-bombers, being in bed at the hotel wasn't a finish to the thing.

It was a never-ending series of climaxes ... when one felt the thing was finished only to be jolted back into it again ... it was that that got one down.

And I saw that was just the same in the matter of air raids. No matter how severe a single air raid is, the lull that comes after it, whether it be for a week, a few days or merely a day, is enough for civilians to regain their poise, to get back to normal. But if instead of intermittent raids an air force was powerful enough not only to bomb the workers in their factories but to assail them as they went home in their buses, bomb them in their homes, bomb them again as they went to work once more in the morning, bomb them again in their factories, morale *would* go. Carried on right round the clock, it would be more than human nature could stand.

My thought wandered off on those lines as we ate our breakfast to the accompaniment of enemy planes overhead.

VII

We had to get back to London to get our stories on the wire, so we climbed into our Press car after breakfast and drove up to town.

It was good to get back in my office again, among familiar surroundings once more. My desk – some pictures I hadn't yet got around to writing captions for – my typewriter, with bits of sticking-plaster over the keys to help me in my efforts to touch type …

I sank down into my chair and took a look at the pile of letters that had accumulated while I had been away.

I opened the one at the top.

It read: 'Please find closed your income tax assessment for the current year …'

PART THREE

Appendix I

Transcript extract from Wallace Reyburn's 1962 Canadian Broadcasting Corporation interview reviewing Terence Robertson's controversial book, *Dieppe: The Shame and the Glory* that labelled some Canadian troops in the Royal Regiment of Canada who took part in the Dieppe Raid cowards.

Presenter: 'One of the most shattering books to reach the Canadian public in many years is a recent one called *The Shame and the Glory: Dieppe*. Written by Terence Robertson, it points the finger of blame at many people in many places. London freelance writer Wallace Reyburn has just finished reading *The Shame and the Glory* and here is his analysis.'

Reyburn: 'Canada's Royal Regiment at Dieppe is certainly shown up in a bad light in this new book about the raid. It would seem reading the book that they are a bunch of cowards scared to get out of their boats on the beach and face the enemy. So scared that they had to be threatened with revolvers to make them go ashore. Such poor soldiers it seems that boats taking off the wounded were besieged by non-wounded and navy men had to beat them off with boathooks to stop the overloaded boats from sinking.

'It's not a very pretty picture and unfortunately there seems no doubt that it's true. But I think Robertson, an Englishman who wrote the book, is being very unfair to the Royals. He gives the impression that elsewhere at Dieppe the Canadians were heroes but at Puys where the Royals landed there was an unhappy story of cowardly conduct.

'To be fair, Robertson should have stressed more strongly the quite different circumstances on the other beaches. For instance I went in with the South Saskatchewan Regiment, the SSRs, at Pourville, They were on the other flank from Puys. I wasn't in the regiment, I was along as a guest for the day as a war correspondent.

'Robertson in his book keeps repeating about the men of the Royals being reluctant to face the enemy. But when he writes of the SSRs at Pourville there is no reluctance to get out of their boats and onto the beach as far as they were concerned. Of course there was no reluctance as the enemy were in their beds when we landed. We went right up the beach without a shot fired at us. We were in the shelter of the sea-wall before the Germans even knew we were there.

'And here's the point I want to make. Supposing the SSRs had been blasted with everything the Germans had when we arrived just like the Royals. Would none of the SSRs have been reluctant to step out into the barrage? I know darn well I would have been very reluctant.

'Robertson should have placed more stress on the essential difference between the different parts of the operation.

'On the main beach, the Essex Scottish and the Hamilton Light Infantry and the French Canadians showed none of the Royals' reluctance. But there the circumstances were quite different. It was a wide beach with space to manoeuvre and shelter up there in the casino if they could make it.

'It was completely different from the Royals, volunteers who had crossed the Atlantic to fight Hitler, having to go into this tiny beach hemmed in by these cliffs that were about 300 feet high. There were pill-boxes and strong points literally right in front of their faces. In the Dieppe Raid the Royals had the dirtiest job of the lot.

'I was over there the other day having another look at Puys beach where they landed. And when I stood there looking at it from the enemy's point of view I could only shake my head. The Royals you see had a dirty job all right. The thing was worse than just a dirty job. It was absolutely ridiculous, foolhardy to the point of being suicidal.

'It was all very well for the planners in the comfort and safety of their planning rooms to set troops a hopeless task like that. It is easy for people who weren't there to start twenty years later inquiring into the moral fibre or lack of it of the soldiers who had to do the job.

'But personally I wouldn't for a second stand in judgment on any member of the Royal Regiment for being hesitant when given as his first taste of battle such a suicidal assignment.

'Well so much for the provocative aspect of *The Shame and the Glory*. As far as the book as a whole is concerned, it is undoubtedly the best of the six books written on Dieppe.

'Almost exactly half the book is devoted to the planning. Robertson has done just the right thing there. Drawing up the plans for Dieppe was one of the monuments of bad planning. And as such it deserves the most thorough and detailed description. It is an object lesson as how the foundations for a disaster can well and truly be laid before an operation ever gets under way.

'The main fault of the book is he hasn't twenty years later taken a good long look back at the raid and presented a well-rounded-out assessment of the whole thing. He has made it his business just to present the facts and he does that very well indeed. The facts in some cases aren't enough – they need to be interpreted and assessed.

'Like the fact the Royals were flinching on the beach at Puys and the South Saskatchewans were going up their beach without a moment's hesitation. He should have stressed it's easy to be a hero when you aren't in danger. And also pointed out that many a hero is a coward lucky enough not to be found out.

'And another thing. The reluctant Royals at Puys were without the benefit of their colonel. His boat had been held up for about twenty minutes behind them. They were raw troops without their leader. Robertson should have brought out the fact it is only human nature for inexperienced men to tend to panic when nobody seems to be in charge.

'When the SSRs reached that bridge where Colonel Merritt won his VC, the first men trying to get across were slaughtered. The rest of them held back in the shelter of shops and houses very reluctant. I know because I was there being reluctant with them.

'But then along came Colonel Merritt. At once he rallied them and inspired them with his own special brand of courage and leadership. All of a sudden they became an organized fighting force and they followed him across the bridge without any hesitation at all.'

Presenter: Wallace Reyburn with a review of the book *The Shame and the Glory.*

Appendix II

Wallace Reyburn's 1967 Dieppe letter to the *Sunday Telegraph* newspaper attacking Lord Mounbatten and his fellow planners responsible for the Dieppe Raid on the twenty-fifth anniversary of the disastrous military operation.

Sunday Telegraph August 27, 1967

Where Lord Mounbatten's planners went astray

I feel I really must say something on behalf of those who unlike Admiral of the Fleet Earl Mountbatten were at Dieppe twenty-five years ago. At the anniversary ceremony, he spoke of the valuable lessons learned from the raid, one of which was 'a strongly defended port cannot be profitably seized by direct assault'.

But why, to use a Canadian expression, did we have to learn it the hard way? It would have been thought that all those 'valuable lessons' were things Lord Mountbatten's planners could have figured out for themselves without the sacrifice of 1,137 lives.

For example, was it necessary to expose troops to the criminal farce of trying to take massive concrete forts merely with two-inch mortars and Sten guns in order to learn it just doesn't work?

Tank drivers were asked to drive their tanks up a steep pebbled beach, through gaps blown in a sea-wall then across a broad esplanade fully exposed to the heavy guns on the cliffs before being able to reach the relative security of the narrow streets of the town. None succeeded in making the journey. Surely the planners could have seen it was asking the impossible?

Likewise the planners, aided by intelligence, could surely have foreseen it was asking too much of troops to ask them to cross the River Scie, which lies between Pourville and Dieppe itself, in the circumstances in which they found themselves, i.e. told at that time of year it was a mere trickle in a dried-up riverbed, they arrived to find the river in flood.

In the same way one would have thought the planners could have figured it out that it would be foolhardy to the point of being suicidal for a whole battalion of the left flank at Puys to get through a gap only a couple of hundred yards wide in the cliffs, with the Germans entrenched in forts on either side.

The key to the whole plan was Surprise. The real reason there was no softening up of the area by air bombardment was that the planners pinned their faith on catching the enemy unawares. Bombardment beforehand would have alerted them.

Now surprise is a frequently used if *not* the essential part of a military raid. The very word 'raid' connotes in and out before the enemy quite knows what is happening.

That is fine when a small number of raiders is used at a single point. But it was a pure pipe dream on the part of the planners to expect to achieve complete surprise when launching 5,000 men in 300 ships on a front more than five miles wide. In the event those of us on the right flank did achieve perfect surprise, getting ashore and in among the houses before a shot was fired at us.

But unfortunately, while our ships were crossing the Channel in the middle of the night, the bulk of them, to our left, encountered a German convoy sneaking down the Channel. A miniature naval battle ensued and this held up that part of our convoy. By then we on the right flank had woken everybody up and the remainder of our troops arrived to find the Germans alerted and ready for them. The result was slaughter.

But Mountbatten's planners were not through yet. So much faith did they have in their plan that they made no allowance for it to be altered if things went wrong. The commander in the field, the Canadian General Roberts, was not allowed to do the logical thing that suggested itself to the man on the spot – with the central assault a shambles, switch the reserve troops to the right flank, where a foothold had been established. Instead he had to adhere rigidly to the plan and go against one of the oldest axioms of war (Never reinforce failure) by throwing more troops into the shocking mess on the main beach at Dieppe.

To paraphrase a well-known saying, it was 'back to the old planning room' for Mountbatten's men, and they did in the end get it right. But the Dieppe plan was like one of the more fanciful socialist experiments thought up by Labour party planners – wonderful on paper but a fiasco in practice. With the saddening difference that an appalling loss of life was involved.

WALLACE REYBURN
London N.W.3.

Mr Reyburn, a war correspondent at Dieppe, was 'not by choice but by chance' on one of the first landing craft to touch down and in the last ship to leave the scene. His book on the raid, *Rehearsal for Invasion*, was a wartime best-seller.

Appendix III

On 27 March 1980, the *Birmingham Post*, the leading regional English daily newspaper covering the West Midlands, published Wallace Reyburn's review of Ronald Atkin's book, *Dieppe 1942: The Jubilee Disaster* (Macmillan).

Secret documents reveal the disaster at Dieppe

The Dieppe Raid in 1942 was a classic failure of the Second World War. WALLACE REYBURN, who received the OBE after being the only war correspondent to go ashore at Dieppe, reviews a new book on the subject:

Having read a dozen books on the subject including my own, I did not think Robert Atkin could make his new offering fresh and readable. But it is, thanks mainly to the fact that he has the advantage over most of the earlier writers on the subject.

Quentin Reynolds, of *Collier's*, A.B. Austin of the old *Herald* and I, who had covered the raid for the *Montreal Standard*, wrote our books under wartime censorship and were forced to withhold much of which we would have been outspoken about – like, for instance, the intelligence had told us the River Scie would be a dried-up river bed at that time of year and we arrived there to find it in full flood.

Other authors did not have available to them many secret documents, British and German, relating to the affair which have now been placed at the disposal of Atkin.

He made the most of this advantage with a thoroughly researched piece of work, not just dully factual but with a keen eye for the human and humorous aspects. Such as a German officer billeted in the Grand Hotel thinking they were going to be overrun by invaders and deciding to burn his unit's records – so copiously did he soak the documents in petrol that when he put a match to them burned down the entire hotel.

Mention of Quentin Reynolds, much revered by the British for his wartime broadcasts, reminds me that there was much of the phoney about that gentleman. He was not one of the 22 accredited war correspondents, but he horned in on the raid, devoting much of his time to getting drunk in the wardroom of the headquarters destroyer *Calpe*, offshore.

After the raid he approached me and Ross Munro, Canadian Press correspondent, told us he was writing a book on it, could he have a look at our clippings? In the book I was interested to read that he had bumped into me coming off the beaches, had said 'How was it, Wally?' and I had replied – to the extent of ten or a dozen pages of the book. Similarly with Munro. Thus do some people write books.

Can one complain? No, because there is an old axiom in the book writing game: 'If you lift from one writer that's plagiarism but if you lift from two or more – that's research.'

The Dieppe Raid was on August 19, 1942. It was masterminded by Earl Mountbatten's Combined Operations. The idea was to make a large-scale show of activity across the Channel to appease the Russians, who felt they were carrying the brunt of the war in Europe on their front.

Technically 'a reconnaissance in force', involving 6,000 men, it was a frontal attack on Dieppe in daylight. The Canadian Second Division and British Commando units would be conveyed across the Channel in 300 ships and start operations at dawn, take over the port, do as much damage to vital installations as possible, and then return to England. There would be no previous naval or aerial bombardment to soften up the objective – so as not to kill French people and block streets with debris which would impede the Churchill tanks that were to be landed. Success would depend entirely on surprise.

Planned

The raid had originally been planned for July and been cancelled because of bad weather. Did reviving it in August mean that news was leaked to the Germans? The raid was a disaster, only 1,600 returning. Was that because the Germans knew we were coming? Many critics afterwards were of that opinion, but it was not so.

I was attached to the South Saskatchewan Regiment, who landed right on schedule at Pourville. Such a well-kept secret was our arrival that as our landing craft came onto the beach with not a sound to be heard but from our engines and the lapping of the waves, someone remarked: 'If there are a couple of lovers having a bit of fun on the beach, they are going to get one hell of a surprise.'

What went wrong? On the way over in the middle of the night the left flank of our 300 boats bumped into a convoy of German naval vessels sneaking down the Channel. There was an exchange of fire. This held up part of the convoy and the troops on those boats arrived at Dieppe twenty minutes late. By then we on the right flank were ashore and fighting in the streets.

We woke up everybody in the area and even though those in command of the German convoy did not realize and did not alert the Dieppe defences we were making a mini invasion, the German soldiers at their coastal guns were aroused and ready for latecomers and mowed them down as they tried to get ashore.

It is pleasing to know that the mighty German military machine could on occasion be just as inefficient as we so often are. Besides such semi-farce as the naval man burning down his hotel, Atkin tells of a more serious German inefficiency such as that of the vaunted 10th Panzers, a much-vaunted formation, who were in reserve near Rouen ready for just such an eventuality as the Dieppe Raid. Except that they weren't ready.

About to set off for Dieppe, it was found they had no maps of the area and a dispatch rider had to make an 80-mile trip to Lille to get them. Eventually under way, 'the journey to the coast was marred by overheating engines, punctures and breakdowns' and the 15th Army

HQ afterwards were to reprimand them for 'a speed of advance no better than the rate of movement of a bicycle formation'.

Thank God for that, one can say now, because when the signal came for us to withdraw we had to wait for the navy to come in to the beaches and take us off and as Atkin quotes me in the book: 'It was a classic scene for a movie. We were waiting for the boats and a Panzer division was coming the other way. Who would get there first?'

Who was to blame for the fiasco? Not the Canadian troops. Atkin quotes *The New York Times*: 'Brave men died without hope for the sake of proving that there is a wrong way to invade.' The planners were undoubtedly ultra-optimistic in thinking that a raiding force could take on a fully fortified enemy head-on in daylight and come off best.

They learned – the hard way, with a shocking sacrifice of life – that it can't be done. So Mulberry was developed and we took our own port across the Channel when the major invasion came.

It is interesting that no movie has ever been made of the Dieppe Raid, despite the fact that every campaign, battle and other raid you can think of in the Second World War has been filmed, some of them several times. I once put the idea to a movie company and they said, 'No, thanks. People aren't interested in failure.' I couldn't resist saying, 'What about the Charge of the Light Brigade?'

Appendix IV

On March 17, 1990, the *Birmingham Post* newspaper based in the UK's second largest city, ran another feature on the Dieppe Raid by Wallace Reyburn marking the publication of Brian Loring Villa's book *Unauthorised Action: Mountbatten and the Dieppe Raid* (Oxford University Press).

Dieppe: view from the front

Lord Mountbatten is blamed for the disastrous Dieppe Raid in a new book by a young Canadian academic. London-based writer WALLACE REYBURN, who was awarded the OBE after being the only war correspondent to get ashore at Dieppe, recalls the mood of those who took part.

In his book on the Dieppe Raid, author Brian Loring Villa maintains that the plan prepared by Lord Mountbatten's Combined Operations was a bad one that should have not been accepted by those who put it into effect and he claims that Mountbatten went ahead without the required permission.

As far as the latter accusation is concerned, I wouldn't know, not having seen the papers on which the author bases his contention. But, in regard to whether or not it was a bad plan ...

It is all very well to examine a situation from the cold light of almost half a century later and say that so-and-so should not have done such-and-such. One must bear in mind the mood of the people concerned.

In 1942 the Russians, with some justification, were nagging the Allies to open a Second Front to relieve the pressure on them.

Tobruk and Singapore had fallen, our Murmansk and Atlantic convoys were suffering huge losses, so that our political and military leaders felt something must be done to boost our morale. And – not the least consideration – the Canadians stationed in Britain were screaming for action.

A hundred and fifty thousand Canadians had been parked on the South East coast for two years and were bored with going on military 'exercises', hanging around pubs and doing the odd bit of womanizing. It rankled with them that other Commonwealth countries had long been in the thick of it.

So when the scheme came along for some of them to go into action – any sort of action – they leapt at it.

I was among them out in the Channel bound for we didn't know where and it was revealed that the target was Dieppe.

When the plan was outlined and it amounted to units landing on the flanks and joining up with those going straight into the port, raising a Union Flag on the town hall and then coming home, nobody said 'What the hell's the point of doing *that*!' Nobody observed that there had been a specific purpose to raids such as those on places like St Nazaire (to put the submarine base out of action).

It was explained that this was not actually a raid but a 'reconnaissance in force' to see whether it was possible to succeed in frontally attacking a defended port. Oh, I see. Let's go.

Foolhardy

That was the mood, Nobody stopped to point out that you did not need to sacrifice thousands of lives to prove such an endeavour was impractical.

Everything was based on the element of surprise. There was no softening up of Dieppe with bombardment.

We went in cold to catch them with their pants down. And on the right flank at Pourville, where I was lucky enough to be, we did.

A measure of our achievement of surprise was the remark of one of the soldiers as our landing craft approached the shore at dawn: 'If there's a couple having a bit of you-know-what on the beach they're going to get one hell of a shock.'

Even the racket of our army boots on the huge pebbles on the beach failed to wake up the Germans.

We cut through the barbed wire along the top of the sea-wall and made our way into the town before there was any sign of activity from the enemy. The support battery behind us landed successfully except for at least one unfortunate casualty.

It was a Canadian Scottish regiment and it was really moving to see their piper standing on the top of the sea-wall piping them ashore, until there was the mournful moaning as a bullet punctured his bagpipes.

The French were thrilled to see us after the humiliation of German occupation but they were warned not to go over the top about our arrival.

Leaflets were dropped telling them it was not the Second Front, just a raid.

I saw one man scooping up leaflets and remarked to a local that he seemed eager to spread the warning. He shook his head and with vivid sign language indicated the dire shortage of toilet paper.

A little French boy thoroughly enjoyed our visit. He spent the day putting his beret at the end of a stick and poking it out cowboy style around the edge of a building and if nobody fired he knew it was safe to dart across the street. At least I hoped he spent the whole day doing it. Thanks to catching the Germans unawares, the Canadians at Pourville were able to penetrate more than a mile inland.

If the same sort of surprise had been achieved on the left flank perhaps the Dieppe story would have been different and Mountbatten could have been lauded as some sort of genius of strategy.

But, sadly, the Canadians going in at Puys on that flank were delayed for 20 minutes when the boats taking them bumped into a Germany convoy sneaking down the Channel.

So, instead of arriving like us, they got there in broad daylight with everyone on shore wide awake from our landing on the other flank, with ghastly results. That delay threw the whole operation out of kilter. And that bit of bad luck was one of the main reasons for the Dieppe Raid becoming a shambles.

I felt sorry for the unfortunately nicknamed Maj-Gen J. H. 'Ham' Roberts, head of the Canadian Second Division and thus Army Commander at Dieppe. He was made the scapegoat.

Shortly after the raid he was removed from command of field units and put in charge of replacement and training units and eventually given a War Graves Commission post.

At the height of the battle Roberts had pleaded with Combined Ops that the French-Canadian battalion, Les Fusiliers Mont-Royal, held in reserve to go in at the main beach, should be switched to Pourville.

Any fool could see that you don't reinforce failure but instead support success. But Combined Ops would have none of it. Mountbatten's master plan had to be adhered to.

When the raid was all over Combined Ops listed among their 'Lessons Learned': 'The Military plan must be flexible to enable the Commander to apply force where force has already succeeded.' Brilliant!

Survivors

My personal contact with Roberts was brief. During the withdrawal I got into three boats which in succession sank, so I was thankful when I was able to swim to the *Calpe*, General Roberts' headquarters destroyer.

When I asked Roberts when we'd be leaving, he said: 'I am not leaving until every possible survivor is picked up.'

This meant we spent more than three hours going back and forth along the shore, constantly shelled and dive-bombed, before heading for home with the decks and cabins heaped with wounded, exhausted survivors plucked from the sea.

I realized then what a good and conscientious commander Roberts had been. And for such decisions Mountbatten saw he was demoted.

Daily Telegraph   July 13, 2001

Wallace Reyburn
The biographer of Thomas Crapper

WALLACE REYBURN, who has died aged 87, wrote *Flushed with Pride* (1969), the hugely successful biography of Thomas Crapper (1837-1910), the man who invented the modern flush lavatory.

Deftly pitched between the informative and the tongue-in-cheek, the book was hailed as "a classic of the smallest room". Learned digressions on "valveless water-waste preventers" were interspersed with the story of an 11-year-old Yorkshire boy who walked to London looking for work and ended up plumber "By Appointment" to Edward VII.

Among other things, Reyburn revealed that Crapper fitted out Sandringham for Queen Victoria and made a royal blue velvet armchair lavatory for Edward VII's mistress Lily Langtry at her house in Hampstead. Crapper himself expired after leaving his sick bed to mend a faulty cistern.

Although Reyburn carefully eschewed the easy laugh, at first some people concluded that the book must be a hoax. It wasn't; but his follow-up effort, *Bust-Up — The Uplifting Tale of Otto Titzling and the Development of the Bra* (1971), was pure fiction. This did not prevent the creators of "Trivial Pursuit" naming Titzling as the creator of the brassière in an answer to one of their questions.

Wallace Reyburn was born in Auckland, New Zealand, on July 3 1913, the son of a dentist. He was sent to England as a boarder at Berkhamsted School, Hertfordshire, and on his return home became a journalist with the *New Zealand Herald*. He came back to England to cover the 1935-36 New Zealand rugby union tour. Afterwards, he remained in Europe, later moving to Canada to become managing editor of a magazine.

During the war he worked as a war correspondent with the Canadian Army and in 1942 was the only

Reyburn: forsook the easy laugh

journalist to go ashore in the ill-fated Dieppe raid. The 10th man ashore when the first assault party landed at Pourville, he witnessed the heavy fighting for six hours before escaping back to England in a destroyer which he only reached after two of the landing craft in which he had set out had been sunk. His first book *Rehearsal for Invasion* recalled the raid and became a bestseller.

Reyburn returned to Britain in 1950 as London columnist for the *Toronto Telegram*. He wrote 25 books including *Frost — Anatomy of a Success*, a biography of David Frost, and an acclaimed biography of the radio personality and wit, Gilbert Harding. He also wrote several books about rugby — *The Unsmiling Giants* was about the 1967 All Blacks' tour of Britain — and helped the former newsreader Reginald Bosanquet with his memoirs *Let's Get Through Wednesday*. Reyburn was appointed OBE for his part in the Dieppe raid.

He married, in 1946, Betty Munro. They had two sons and a daughter. His wife and daughter predeceased him.

Appendix VI

The Times 14 July 2001

WALLACE REYBURN

Eyewitness to the Dieppe Raid whose writing career later went down the drain

Reyburn, flanked by an army photographer and another journalist, arrives back in Britain after the Dieppe Raid; below, his most successful book

The New Zealand-born writer Wallace Reyburn distinguished himself with two markedly different works of prose. As a war reporter in 1942, he made it ashore during the Dieppe Raid, where he witnessed and later described how 84 Canadian soldiers were killed and 89 forced to surrender. For his efforts he was appointed OBE, and the resulting book (his first), *Rehearsal for Invasion* (1943), was hailed as a moving account of the ill-fated operation.

Reyburn would go on to write books on such diverse topics as rugby, Gilbert Harding, David Frost and bras, but it was to be his 1969 volume *Flushed With Pride, The Story of Thomas Crapper* for which he became best known. It fuelled the myth that the inventor of the flush lavatory went by the name of Crapper — and that it was he who gave the language the slang word associated with the device.

In truth, although there was a Yorkshire-born plumber called Thomas Crapper, who from 1861 to 1904 ran a successful London-based company selling sanitary wares, he did not invent the modern lavatory and made no substantial advances in sanitation.

A water closet had been designed by Sir John Harington as long ago as 1596 and in 1775 Alexander Cumming patented the first flush lavatory to use a curved soil pipe filled with water. Reyburn's work acknowledged these forerunners, but mischievously exaggerated Crapper's influence on subsequent developments.

The most significant product he attributed to Crapper, the "Silent Valveless Water Waste Preventer", a syphonic discharge system that allowed a lavatory to flush effectively when the cistern was only half-full, was actually patent-

ed by one Albert Giblin in 1898. It has been suggested that Crapper bought the patent rights from Giblin, who may have been his employee, and marketed it himself. At any event, it was Crapper who was called in to supply the very latest in sanitation to Queen Victoria at Sandringham House. And it is Crapper who is commemorated, albeit by a man-hole cover, in Westminster Abbey to this day.

Flushed With Pride was full of genial erudition, and written in a wry, dead-pan manner that left readers unsure whether the whole thing was a

![FLUSHED WITH PRIDE. The Story of THOMAS CRAPPER]

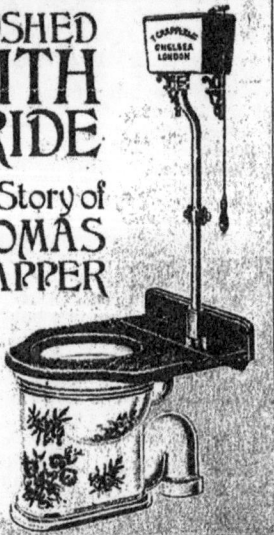

hoax. The book featured illustrations rich in *Carry On*-style innuendo — the "Down-Right Cock" tap and the "Climax Relief Valve" — and implausibly suggested that on his deathbed Crapper, tormented by a faulty loo, "got from his bed and crept into the bathroom. His practised fingers soon found the flaw in the mechanism, the toilet was flushed and he returned to his bed ... he then died, a dedicated craftsman to the end."

Suspicions that Reyburn might be a professional legpuller were confirmed in 1971 when he published *Bust-Up*, a

vivid but entirely fictitious account of how the brassière had been invented by a fellow called Otto Titzling.

The son of an Auckland dentist, Wallace Macdonald Reyburn was a boarder at Berkhamsted School in Hertfordshire. After returning home to work on the *New Zealand Herald*, he came to England again to cover the 1935-36 New Zealand rugby tour. After travelling in Europe and Canada, he joined the *Montreal Standard* as a war correspondent.

With the Dieppe raid intended partly to publicise the Canadian contribution to the war effort, the presence of journalists was vital. Reyburn came ashore with the South Saskatchewans at Pourville, accompanied by two members of the army film and photographic unit.

Unfortunately, the main part of the battalion was landed on the wrong side of the Scie estuary and came under heavy mortar fire as it crossed by the only bridge. Reyburn lost his photographers, but managed to find cover in a house, from which he observed for six-and-a-half hours the raging battle. Most harrowingly, he saw the remnants of the battalion make a dash from the cover of the sea wall for the boats arriving to evacuate them. Many were killed by machinegun fire. Reyburn himself escaped in a destroyer after being in two landing craft that were sunk.

After the war he settled in North London, where he continued to write. He penned a biography of David Frost, *Frost — Anatomy of a Success* (1968) and, in 1979, *Gilbert Harding: A Candid Portrayal*. There were novels, too, and several rugby companions, including *The Unsmiling Giants* (1968), which covered the 1967 All Blacks tour of Britain, and *A History of Rugby* (1971).

But it was his ingenious life of Crapper that brought him his greatest success. To it may be traced the now widespread belief that the English language derived one of its more potent vulgarisms from the good Yorkshire name of a Victorian plumber. The real derivation is obscure, but the word *crappe*, meaning chaff or any other waste material, emerged in the 13th century.

There was truth, however, in Reyburn's suggestion that the fame of Crapper owed something to US troops passing through Britain in the First World War. Most were farm boys, unfamiliar with the marvels of urban hygiene. Overawed by Crapper's splendid wares, they made delighted play of the maker's name serendipitously emblazoned on them. This, or something like it, is what etymologists call a back formation.

Delighted by the furore his book on Crapper had caused, he determined to write an apparently factual book that was actually pure fantasy. The result was *Bust-Up* (1971), the uplifting tale of how Otto Titzling and his associate Hans Delving designed and developed the bra. The teutonic inventors promoted their creation with a catchy slogan — "Women's busts come in four basic sizes. Small, medium, large, and *mein Gott!*" — only to have the patent stolen from them by the fiendish Philippe de Brassière. This book, too, left some readers flummoxed. In the early 1990s "Otto Titzling" was reputedly required as the correct answer to a question about the inventor of the bra in the board game *Trivial Pursuit*.

Reyburn's daughter and his wife Betty predeceased him. He is survived by his two sons.

Wallace Reyburn, OBE, author, was born on July 3, 1913. He died on June 20, 2001, aged 87.

Appendix VII

Theme from Dieppe Concerto

War correspondents don't normally compose music to evoke their battle experiences. But Canadian war correspondent Wallace Reyburn with the help of pianist/composer Paul de Marky produced *Theme from Dieppe Concerto*, evoking his harrowing experience in what proved Canada's equivalent of *The Charge of the Light Brigade* in terms of courage facing impossible odds.

The five pages of sheet music arranged by de Marky were published by Gordon V. Thompson in 1945 and sold for 50 cents.

Ross Reyburn dug up a copy of this long-forgotten document from his father's possessions and asked his former newspaper colleague, veteran *Birmingham Post* music critic Christopher Morley, to give his verdict on the composition.

No doubt Wallace Reyburn would be flattered to find a highly regarded music critic, who has covered CBSO [City of Birmingham Orchestra] concerts including the celebrated Simon Rattle era for more than 40 years, praising his long-forgotten composition (see below).

Wallace Reyburn's Dieppe Concerto is a unique example of a genre popular in film music during the mid-1940s, when miniature imitations of Rachmaninov piano concertos conveyed both stirring heroism and soaring romantic aspirations; famous examples include The Warsaw Concerto, Cornish Rhapsody, and the Dream of Olwen. The Dieppe Concerto is finely written, generously melodic and powerfully defiant. It differs from its peers in that it was never written as film-music, but came instead from the composer's first-hand experience of reporting on the Normandy landings. It is a moving memorial to those tremendous times.

November 2021. Christopher Morley,
Birmingham Post music critic

Theme from
DIEPPE
CONCERTO

Wallace
Reyburn

arranged by
Paul de Marky

price *50* cents

Gordon V. Thompson Limited – 193 Yonge Street, Toronto

Theme from
DIEPPE CONCERTO

Arr. by
Paul de Marky

WALLACE REYBURN

Theme from Dieppe Concerto–4

Theme from Dieppe Concerto-4

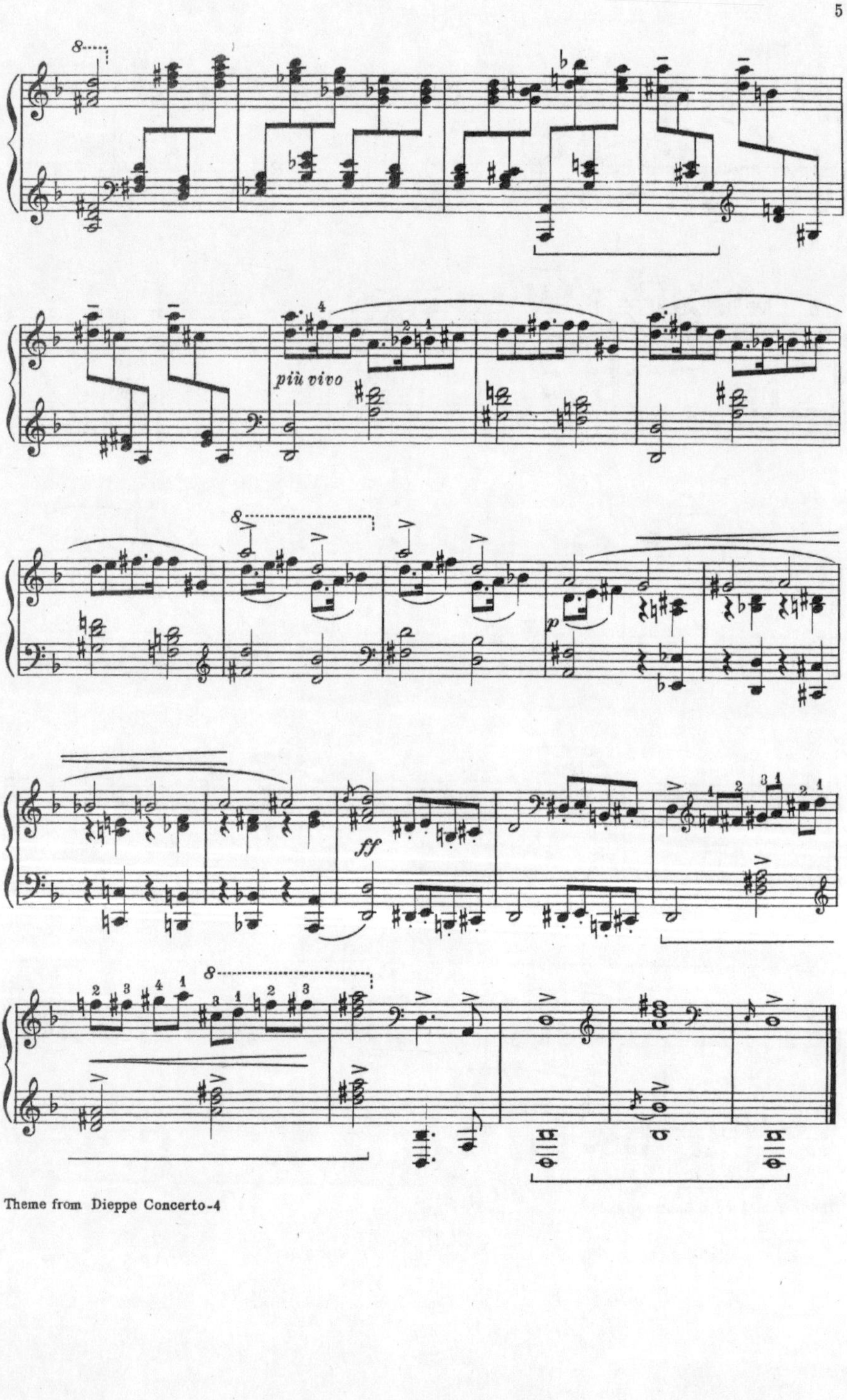

Theme from Dieppe Concerto-4

Appendix VIII

Vive la Dieppe!

Tributes to French residents during the Dieppe Raid from Canadian war correspondent Wallace Reyburn in his book *Rehearsal for Invasion* published in 1943 after witnessing the street fighting after following the first troops ashore at Pourville-sur-Mer.

* * *

"We'd been given leaflets to distribute to any French people we encountered... We handed them around, and a boy in his teens read his closely with obvious interest. Then when he was through reading he asked if he could have some more of them. One of the officers gave him a pile... But as he folded the leaflets and put them in his pocket it dawned on me his request for more of them had been prompted not by any spreads-the-news motive, but for the more prosaic fact of France's dire shortage of toilet-paper.

* * *

In the midst of all this noise came another sound that made us fully alive to the homelike atmosphere of our battlefield, which brought suddenly to our minds what it must have been like for the French people living here here to be awakened out of their night's slumber and be confronted with the spectacle of Nazi garrison troops and five thousand Allied visitors fighting out a battle royal in their streets and back gardens. What brought this home to us with a start was that In the midst of this bombardment of noise we heard a sound so familiar that it carried us back suddenly back to everyday life – it was the tinkle of some Frenchman's alarm clock.

* * *

Our group of French friends soon dispersed and returned to their homes when it became known to them we were going to move farther inland. As I watched them return to their homes I couldn't help but feel moved by the way they were taking it all. They kept quite cool and unflustered. There was no stampede for the open country. I didn't see a single Frenchman throughout the whole six and a half hours I was shore, heading out of town.

Since my first meeting with French people earlier in the morning, I'd almost forgotten about them, but, looking about now, It noticed several of them at their windows.

From where I was sitting I could look up the long valley behind the town. On that flat riverside land there were several farms, and near the barn of one of these, about quarter of a mile away, I caught sight of a farmer moving about. I watched him and saw him stroll about his meadow, pause every now and then, and look up at the planes flying by. He seemed quite unaware that the fort on the golf course was firing mortar shells directly over his head at the terraces on the other side of the valley, where detachments of our men had now penetrated.

I saw him bring his four cows in to the relative shelter of the barn and then stroll across the meadow to bring in a pile of hay for them.

This determination to carry on business as usual, was shared by another Frenchman we encountered. An aged fellow wearing no hat and without a shirt underneath his jacket, he apparently had his mind set on having fresh bread for his meals that day. He cycling along the streets on his bicycle. Either he reckoned Nazi snipers would recognise his civilian status or else he had a profound disregard for the likelihood of his being dispatched by a chunk of flying metal – anyway, he was pedalling along gaily, a long French loaf propped up in the basket on the front of his bike.

*　＊　＊　＊*

Most of the French women were staying indoors, down in their cellars for shelter or watching from their windows, But there was a decided inclination on the part of the men, and particularly boys, to be out and about and to get a good view of what was going on.

There was a little French boy who probably got a bigger kick out of the raid than any of us. ...

He was wearing a grey shirt and knickerbockers and a bright blue beret. He dashed hither and thither among our troops, keeping in close touch with every phase of the battle.

I caught sight of him now, across the other side of the square ... I watched him crouch behind a house and take his beret off and project it out on the end of a stick round the edge of the building. No sniper took a pot-shot at it, so he concluded the coast was clear.

He put his beret back on and dashed across the street.

* * *

On the veranda of the big white Albion Hotel I noticed someone moving about.

I said, 'Look out! There's a sniper up there right now.'

The officer looked through his binoculars and burst into a grin. He handed me the glasses. 'Here,' he said, 'have a look at your sniper.'

He turned out to be a rotund, round-faced Frenchman, ... He was strolling up and down the veranda, not the least bit concerned about the commotion that was going on around him. The building a couple away from his was on fire, and part of the roof of his own hotel had been blown away by a shell. But he was walking blithely back and forth and seemed no end pleased at the wonderful ringside box he had.

Appendix IX

Modern Dieppe

Ross Reyburn

The marina complex in modern Dieppe today offers a striking landmark providing sharp contrast to the battle scarred images of the town resulting from the carnage created by disastrous 1942 Allied raid.

Today there is no visible evidence of the trail of destruction created by the battle when 5,000 Canadian troops tried in vain to seize control of Dieppe and Pourville-sur-Mer and Puys, the two small resorts either side of the main town.

The death toll in the raid was not confined to the opposing armies. In Dieppe, thirty-two residents were to lose their lives, including two fifteen-year-old twin boys, while ten civilians were killed in the Pourville area.

However, the Canadian troops who brought war to the town were treated with compassion by the local population. Despite the obvious evidence to the contrary, the Germans claimed the French had taken their side in the raid.

While it was true Louis-Marie Poullain, the editor of the local newspaper La Vigie (The Lookout), supported France's Vichy government, most of Dieppe kept their heads down hoping for the day their town would be free of their German oppressors.

On 1 September 1944, the 2nd Division of the Canadian army, including survivors of the ill-fated raid two years earlier, made a symbolic diversion from the main Allied advance, revisiting the town receiving a rapturous welcome. Happily, the Germans had retreated deciding not to defend the town.

There is no shortage of well designed memorials and plaques commemorating the bravery of the Canadians. Le Mémorial du 19 Août 1942, the museum dedicated to the raid, is housed in a nineteenth-century Italianate theatre in the town. Not far away are sighted the memorials on the promenade by the town's pebble beach where the main landings took place and these include a moving tribute to the soldiers in Les Fusiliers Mont-Royal regiment mowed down in a futile later attack on the main beach.

In the town itself at the western end of the beach esplanade lies a small park called Square du Canada (Canada Square). There you can find the distinctive Dieppe-Canada Monument while the wall behind contains a plaque commemorating the Dieppe Raid.

The plaque inscription offers an insight into why the residents of Dieppe area have not forgotten the brave Canadians who lost their lives after leaving safety of their homeland to fight the Germans who had taken over the town on the Normandy coast. Translated the inscription reads:

> *On the 19th of August 1942*
> *on the beaches of Dieppe*
> *our Canadian cousins*
> *marked with their blood*
> *the road to our final liberation*
> *foretelling thus their victorious*
> *return on September 1, 1944.*

The deeds of Canadians soldiers landing on the two small resorts, Pourville-sur-Mer and Puys flanking the main resort are also stylishly commemorated.

In Pourville, the small bridge spanning the River Scie was renamed Lieutenant Colonel Ces Merritt's Bridge in honour of Canada's first VC on the war. A wooden information board with a photo of Merritt details his heroics repeatedly leading his troops across the bridge ignoring heavy enemy fire with the rallying cry: "Come on over, there's nothing to worry about here."

In Puys, a plaque remembers the terrible slaughter of the men of Royal Regiment of Canada directed ashore after dawn broke on a narrow beach overlooked by daunting cliffs manned by the enemy.

Just over three miles from the town lies the immaculately kept Canadian War Cemetery in the village of Hautot-sur-Mer. Its distinctive back to back-to-back headstones contain the identified graves of 582 Canadian soldiers.

The fact three in ten Canadians speak French as their first language through the province of Quebec's historic links with France partially explains why the residents of Dieppe have not forgotten the raid.

Another factor is the Allies mounted no bomber or heavy artillery bombardment endangering the lives of the local population or reducing the town's infrastructure to rubble. The fact my father witnessing six hours of street fighting in Pourville saw no residents heading for safety out of town and Canadian soldiers were given their chocolate rations as well as propaganda leaflets to the French they encountered evidenced the sense of camaraderie experienced in their encounters with the local population.

While the Dieppe Raid ranks as the major event in the town's history, the Normandy port by the English Channel is not short of other happier claims to fame. With the nearest beach to Paris, it became France's first bathing resort in the 19th century with a casino adding to its appeal as a tourist destination situated on an attractive cliff-strewn coastline.

Famous for its scallops with a regular ferry service to Newhaven the other side of the English Channel, today's Dieppe has more than 700 moorings and berths in its attractive marina complex with three basins just inside the mouth of the river Arques free of tidal restrictions.

The town's Saturday market with its huge array of fresh produce was voted France's finest market on national television in 2020 while the town's International Kite Festival held every two years ranks as one of the world's largest kite festivals.

While Dieppe doesn't match the sun soaked appeal and night life of France's major Mediterranean resorts, it outmatches the country's the more glamorous southern coastal resorts in one important respect..

In the Château-Musée de Dieppe housed in the impressive 15th century castle on a hillside overlooking the town, tribute is paid to the town's heritage as The Painter's Resort in the 19th century.

The long roll call of famous artists attracted to the area with its striking coastline included J. M. W. Turner (1775–1851), Eugene Boudin (1824–1898) Camille Pissarro (1830–1903) Claude Monet (1840–1926), Paul Gaugin (1840–1903) and Walter Sickert (1860–1942).

Their paintings provide a vivid reminder today of the town's impressive artistic legacy. Just a short drive from my Birmingham home there is a striking reminder of the Dieppe Raid in the impressive art deco Barber Institute of Fine Arts on the University of Birmingham campus.

Walk up the wide circular marble staircase to the main gallery and you can view Claude Monet's evocative painting L'Eglise de Varengeville (The Church at Varengeville). Sixty years after it was painted in 1882, it was this daunting cliffside setting that provided the one unqualified success of the Dieppe Raid when Lord Lovat's commandos successfully destroyed the formidable German gun battery placed at Varengeville guarding Dieppe.

Bibliography

Bishop, Patrick, *Operation Jubilee: Dieppe, 1942: The Folly and the Sacrifice* (Penguin Viking, 2021)

Churchill, Winston, *The History of the Second World War: Volume 4 – The Hinge of Fate* (Cassell, 1951)

Hamilton, Nigel, *The Full Monty – Volume 1: Montgomery of Alamein 1887–1942* (Allen Lane, 2001)

Munro, Ross, *Gauntlet to Overlord: The Story of the Canadian Army* (Macmillan of Canada, 1945)

Robertson, Terence, *Dieppe: The Shame and the Glory* (Pan, 1962)

Smith, Adrian, *Mountbatten: Apprentice Warlord 1900–1943* (I.B. Tauris, 2010)

Thompson, R. W., *Dieppe at Dawn – The Story of the Dieppe Raid* (Hutchinson, 1956)

Villa, Brian Loring, *Unauthorised Action: Mountbatten and the Dieppe Raid* (Oxford University Press, 1990)

Zuehlke, Mark, *Tragedy at Dieppe: Operation Jubilee, August 19, 1942* (Douglas & McIntyre, 2012)

Index